# THE SUFFRAGISTS

TO the Honourable the Speaker and Members of the House of Representatives in Parliament assembled.

THE Petition of the undersigned Women, of the age of twenty-one years and upwards, resident in the Colony of New Zealand, humbly sheweth :—

THAT large numbers of Women in the Colony have for several years petitioned Parliament to extend the franchise to them.

THAT the justice of the claim, and the expediency of granting it, was, during the last Session of Parliament, affirmed by both Houses ; but, that for reasons not affecting the principle of Women's Franchise, its exercise has not yet been provided for.

THAT if such provision is not made before the next General Election, your petitioners will, for several years, be denied the enjoyment of what has been admitted by Parliament to be a just right, and will suffer a grievous wrong.

THEY therefore earnestly pray your Honourable House to adopt such measures as will enable Women to record their votes for Members of the House of Representatives at the ensuing General Election.

THEY further pray that your Honourable House will pass no Electoral Bill which shall fail to secure to Women this privilege.

And your petitioners, as in duty bound, will ever pray, &c.

| NAME. | ADDRESS. |
|---|---|
| Mary. J. Carpenter | Yaldhurst |
| Annie Gilberthorpe | Yaldhurst |
| Susann Clarkson | Hornby |
| Julia F. Shelton | Hornby. |
| Jane F. Smithie | Johnston |
| Isabella Chaplin | Templeton |
| Mary Hansen | Templeton |
| Lovise Rosendale | Templeton |
| Priscilla Marshall | Templeton |
| Margaret Watson | Templeton |
| Ester Haktte | Templeton |
| Jessie Gudsell | Templeton |
| Julia Haiess | Templeton |

*The prayer for the 1893 suffrage petition. Women's suffrage supporters, who had come close to victory on several occasions previously, were determined to win this time.*

# THE SUFFRAGISTS

*Women Who
Worked for the Vote*

*Essays from The Dictionary
of New Zealand Biography*

*With an Introduction
by Dorothy Page*

BRIDGET WILLIAMS BOOKS

DICTIONARY OF NEW ZEALAND BIOGRAPHY

Jointly published in 1993 by Bridget Williams Books Limited,
PO Box 11-294, Wellington, New Zealand, and the Dictionary of
New Zealand Biography / Department of Internal Affairs,
PO Box 805, Wellington, New Zealand.

ISBN 0 908912 38 2

Design by Mission Hall Design Group
Typeset by Archetype, Wellington
Printed by South Wind Production Pte Ltd, Singapore

*The Dictionary of New Zealand Biography* gratefully
acknowledges the assistance of the General Fund of the
New Zealand Lottery Grants Board.

# CONTENTS

## BIOGRAPHIES

# PREFACE

*The Suffragists* grew out of a desire to mark Suffrage Year 1993 by making known the lives of those New Zealand women who were responsible for winning the vote in 1893. Selected from *The Dictionary of New Zealand Biography*, these 28 essays about suffragists represent a cross-section of women involved in the suffrage movement. They include lone figures who spoke out in favour of women's suffrage long before it was a popular cause, leaders of the organised campaign for the vote, supporters who were not prominent in the movement but who worked hard behind the scenes, and writers who sought to influence public opinion on the issue through their newspaper articles, novels and poems. Many of these women continued to work for equal rights and allied themselves with feminist and humanitarian causes and organisations after the vote was won. The introductory essay gives a context for their lives.

This book was a team effort. The *Dictionary* is indebted to the authors who liked the idea and agreed to their essays being published here. We are especially grateful to Dorothy Page for her introduction. Publication would not have been possible without the hard work and dedication of *Dictionary* staff who all had a hand in it, and especially a small team who finally brought the various areas of production and picture research together. I thank them all.

*Claudia Orange*
*General Editor*

# EDITORIAL NOTES

For a more detailed explanation of editorial practices readers should refer to *The Dictionary of New Zealand Biography*.

### PERSONAL NAMES

The name used at the head of each biography is generally the fullest formal version of the name by which the subject was best known in New Zealand. Well-documented alternative names appear in the text and index.

### DATES OF BIRTH, DEATH AND MARRIAGE

Dates given in text and headings of biographies have been verified in most cases from certificates of registration or from equally reliable primary sources. When it has not been possible to determine specific dates, uncertainty and the range of possibilities are indicated.

### FURTHER READING

The list which appears at the foot of the introduction and each biography is chiefly intended as a guide to further reading. It also points to some of the major sources used. The location of unpublished material follows its citation. The following library symbols are used to identify location:

| | |
|---|---|
| CMU | The Library, Canterbury Museum, Christchurch |
| CU | The Library, University of Canterbury, Christchurch |
| DUHO | Hocken Library, University of Otago, Dunedin |
| WTU | Alexander Turnbull Library, Wellington |

# INTRODUCTION

'Womanhood Franchise granted!!!' With uncharacteristic
ebullience Catherine Fulton, the dignified matriarch of a
landowning New Zealand family, recorded this in her diary on
19 September 1893. Her exclamation reflected the elation of
women all over the country. When the news came through that
the governor had signed the measure that enfranchised women
there was spontaneous celebration. 'Splendid meeting', ran
the telegraphed account of one gathering, 'City Hall crammed
mostly women enthusiasm unbounded thousand handker-
chiefs waving for victory.'

Women were celebrating not only their enfranchisement
and a major advance towards equality in citizenship, but also
– and even more important to many – the chance to influence
society. New Zealand was the first country in the world to
grant women the vote and congratulations poured in from
suffragists elsewhere: the achievement of New Zealand women
gave 'new hope and life to all women struggling for emancipation'. The campaign for the vote in remote New Zealand was
part of the movement for women's rights in Europe, Britain
and her colonies and the United States.

Two main themes ran through the 'first-wave feminism'
of the late nineteenth century: equal rights for women and
moral reform of society. The equal rights movement had
its origin in the eighteenth century. The philosophers of
the Enlightenment envisaged individual political rights
for men, but the arguments they employed could logically
be extended to women. In 1792 Mary Wollstonecraft, in-
spired by the early French Revolution and especially the
Declaration of the Rights of Man, produced the founding

text of equal-rights feminism, *A vindication of the rights of women.*

Movements for moral reform, and a significant role for women within them, may be traced to the evangelical revival of the later eighteenth and early nineteenth centuries and, beyond that, to a spiritual individualism which stressed the responsibility of all believers, women as well as men, for their own salvation. In both Britain and America, the evangelical revival generated movements and groups aiming at specific social reforms, in an effort to purify society of moral abuses. In these movements, and also in Protestant churches without a strict hierarchical structure, women had enhanced opportunities for participation and even for leadership. There was, too, in such circles, a view of women which stressed their moral character, conferring on them a special moral mission. Both these themes – equal rights and moral reform – influenced the New Zealand women's movement, the first primarily through the writings of John Stuart Mill and through contacts with British feminists; the second largely through the missionary endeavours in New Zealand of the Woman's Christian Temperance Union of the United States of America.

Nearly all the New Zealand suffragists in this collection were of British descent, and would have been acutely aware of recent changes in the perception and role of women in Britain. These changes especially affected middle-class women, then excluded from full participation in the public sphere. Married women challenged the law that subordinated them totally to their husbands, without rights over their property or their children. Single women claimed the right to an education that would fit them to enter the professions. Individual women, such as Florence Nightingale, shattered the myth of the helpless, delicate lady. By the 1860s middle-class women in Britain were organising to claim married women's property rights, expanded career opportunities and the vote.

They found a powerful ally in one of the most distinguished men of the age, John Stuart Mill. Recently elected to the British Parliament, Mill presented a women's petition for suffrage in 1866. He followed this up with a motion to enfranchise women, thereby initiating the first parliamentary debate on the topic. The British suffrage campaign was launched. When in 1869 Mill published *On the subjection of women*, arguing the feminist case in terms of liberal individualism, its impact was immediate and profound, not only in Britain but also in America, Australia and New Zealand.

In 1870 Mill wrote to Mary Müller in Nelson, sending her a copy of his book and congratulating her on the *'excellent* beginning' New Zealand women had made in claiming their rights. Müller's writings as 'Femina' mark the beginning of the women's suffrage movement in New Zealand. The time was right. By the end of the 1860s colonial society had become more settled, prosperous and optimistic. People enjoyed a high standard of living, and a degree of social equality was evidenced – in the case of women – by the self-confident wage bargaining of domestic servants. This was the background to a lively debate in Auckland in 1871–72 when the activist Mary Colclough or 'Polly Plum' – converted to the cause of women's rights, she said, by reading Mill – took on all comers in the columns of the press and in public meetings.

The beginning of the debate coincided with the extension of educational opportunities for New Zealand women. In 1871 Learmonth Dalrymple achieved her twin objectives of a public girls' high school in Dunedin and the admission of women to the new University of Otago. In 1877, the same year in which primary education was made compulsory for both sexes and women were recognised as eligible to vote for and sit on school committees and education boards, Kate Edger in Auckland became the first woman to graduate from the University of New Zealand.

During the 1870s Mary Müller discreetly continued to promote women's suffrage among the many politicians of her acquaintance. It is probably she who persuaded two key political figures, William Fox and Alfred Saunders, to take it up. There is also evidence of the widespread reading of Mill at this time. The Reverend Samuel Edger, for example, bought up all the copies of *On the subjection of women* he could find in

Auckland, to lend them to his friends. Robert Stout, one of the first prominent men to speak publicly on women's suffrage, claimed in 1871 to have been converted by reading Mill's work.

Women ratepayers' voting rights in municipal elections, already recognised in Nelson and Otago, were extended to all the provinces in 1875. It suggests growing support for women's rights as citizens in the wider community during the 1870s: the end of the decade saw the first determined efforts to introduce legislation for the parliamentary franchise. In 1878 and 1879 the temper of the country's lower and upper houses of Parliament – the House of Representatives and the Legislative Council – was notably liberal. In the 1878 session members welcomed an Electoral Bill introduced by Robert Stout, which included a clause to enfranchise women ratepayers. It opened up debate on the whole question. The range of opinion in the House of Representatives was wide: some members totally refused to countenance the idea of women voting at all; as one member put it, 'Woman's Parliament is her home'. Others were prepared to grant the vote to women ratepayers, which Stout justified as a first step; yet others, such as William Fox and James Wallis, would accept only the full enfranchisement of women.

The issue of women's eligibility to stand for Parliament was also raised. This was included in the bill, but removed after much heavy-handed humour about the problems honourable members might have in concentrating on business if there were attractive women in the House, and the prospect of husbands of women members having to stay home to look after their children. An amendment in favour of full adult suffrage for women was also lost but the extension of the vote to women ratepayers was accepted in both houses by a secure majority. That the bill failed to become law was for reasons quite unconnected with the issue of women's suffrage.

After this encouraging beginning expectations among suffragists were high in 1879: the government was headed by John Hall, a steady friend of women's suffrage, and many members of the previous House had been returned. The

Qualification of Electors Bill, which proposed giving women property owners the vote, was introduced. However, it soon became clear that granting the vote to women ratepayers was no longer acceptable. The radicals, who objected to women being enfranchised because of their property rather than their capacity, allied with the conservatives, who objected to their being enfranchised at all. Together they had the clause removed. In 1880 and 1881 further efforts by Wallis to bring in women's suffrage also failed. These attempts between 1878 and 1881 provided a trial run. Parliamentarians took sides on matters of principle, without pressure from the community, so that the debates lacked urgency.

Meanwhile, women's rights in less controversial areas were being extended. Women were enabled to sit on liquor advisory committees in 1881 and in 1885 on charitable aid boards. The right of married women to their own property was guaranteed in 1884. But the question of the parliamentary vote was set aside until the end of the decade.

By the time it was taken up again the situation had changed. Closer links with the United States (symbolised as well as facilitated by the opening of a steamship mail link between Auckland and San Francisco in 1871) were bringing New Zealand into touch with a society in many ways akin to its own, shaped by immigration rather than emigration: a country where women were still outnumbered by men in the more remote areas; a new world crackling with energy. The women's movement was already strongly established, in part stimulated by the anti-slavery movement. By the late nineteenth century America was acknowledged as the leader of international feminism. Women's suffrage had been on the agenda as early as 1848, when the Seneca Falls Convention claimed for women the rights enshrined for men in the Declaration of Independence. But hopes raised during the Civil War were suddenly dashed at its end; in 1866 black men were enfranchised, but no women received the vote. As a result of this experience two national women's suffrage associations were formed. While the suffrage cause was advanced when

Wyoming and Utah enfranchised women in 1869 and 1870 respectively, generally the American women's movement concentrated on social rather than political objectives at this time, laying strong foundations for feminism as a mass movement.

Many of the concerns of American women coincided with those of women in New Zealand, notably anxiety about the widespread abuse of alcohol. The Woman's Christian Temperance Union spread rapidly in America after its foundation in 1874, developing a broad programme of social reform. Its president from 1879, Frances Willard, persuaded members that women should protect their homes and families from liquor by claiming, through the vote, their rightful voice in public affairs. Missionaries of the union were sent abroad in 1885 with this message. Mary Leavitt, who reached Auckland in February, found a receptive audience. Travelling the length of the country, with the assistance of Anne Ward she established branches of the first national women's organisation in New Zealand, the New Zealand Women's Christian Temperance Union. After eight years it would lead the movement for the enfranchisement of women to a successful conclusion.

Women of New Zealand sprang into action in the suffrage cause with alacrity. New Zealand was becoming a mature society in terms of gender balance, urbanisation and industrialisation, but in the 1880s the country entered a period of economic recession which would last to the mid 1890s. In the principal towns problems associated with the Old World – poverty, sexual licence and disorder – were being reproduced. Many New Zealand women blamed alcohol for the ills of society and welcomed a women's organisation that sought to ban it.

The social composition of the New Zealand suffrage movement as a whole has not been analysed, but the 28 women represented in these essays, most of whom were prominent workers for the cause, show the following characteristics. Well over half their number were members of the WCTU, and accepted both its prohibitionist stance and its wider reform programme. Their religious affiliations, where known, were predominantly nonconformist and evangelical – many were Baptists, Congregationalists, Wesleyans or Unitarians – and Presbyterians were strongly represented. Many were comfortably off; a few were wealthy. Several, through the standing of the husband, had a respected status: Anne Ward, the first national president of the WCTU, was the wife of a judge. They were mostly urban women from the four main centres. Their ages in 1893 ranged from mid 20s to mid 70s, and although 16 of them were married women at the time of the suffrage campaign, few were burdened with the care of small children. Of those who were, or had been, in paid employment, the majority were teachers or journalists. Only in the WCTU could these women gain political training and leadership experience.

As in the United States, the WCTU in New Zealand was divided into departments. Most were devoted to charitable activities, such as running soup kitchens, visiting prisons and hospitals, and youth work. The franchise and legislation department headed the suffrage campaign, and in Kate Sheppard, from 1887, it found an ideal leader: a woman without sectarian narrowness, characterised by judgement, tolerance and charm. Her means of action – pamphlets, letters to the press, talks, personal contact with politicians, petitions – were those of overseas suffrage groups, with whom she maintained regular contact. The organisation was always limited by lack of funds, but not the least of Kate Sheppard's talents was making a little money go a long way. Writing in the *Prohibitionist*, she kept women up to date not only on the New Zealand suffrage movement but also those in other countries. The campaign was in no way a one-woman operation, but the personal contribution of Kate Sheppard cannot be too heavily stressed.

Women suffragists in the WCTU sought ties with members of Parliament favourable to their cause. Kate Sheppard found an invaluable ally in the courteous and punctilious John Hall, who led the pro-suffrage group in Parliament and supported the women suffragists outside. Prospects for the cause looked good under the Stout–Vogel ministry (1884–87), in office when the campaign began. Although the liquor lobby opposed women's suffrage, which it viewed as a temperance plot, both government leaders were favourable to it, as was John Ballance, another key member of the ministry. In 1887 Julius Vogel himself introduced a Women's Suffrage Bill which included the right to sit in Parliament. Despite the customary jokes and innuendos about the problems of dealing with ladies in the House, it passed its second-reading vote 41 to 22, only to be defeated at the committee stage by the machinations of its opponents.

It was August 1890 before the matter was raised again. Hall put an unexpected motion in favour of the women's franchise which initiated a full-scale debate, culminating in a division with a majority of 26 in favour. But later in the month, both his Women's Franchise Bill and his amendment to the Electoral Bill failed. The Women's Franchise Bill was introduced late in the session and did not receive sufficient support from ministers to make it viable; the amendment to the Electoral Bill was defeated at a vote taken at 2 a.m. when some supporters were absent and others changed sides. Clearly, more pressure on politicians was needed if women's suffrage was to be secured.

Between 1890 and 1893 the women's suffrage campaign all over New Zealand gained momentum. WCTU women determined to broaden the base of their movement by drawing in non-temperance women, working-class women, the educated élite, and women in more isolated areas. They supported Women's Franchise Leagues, which had no temperance connection, and organised massive petitions, open for signature by all adult women. The debate on women's suffrage was particularly intense in Dunedin where the movement had energetic leaders and organisers in Harriet Morison, Marion Hatton and Helen Nicol. Dunedin canvassers for the suffrage petitions consistently – and by a wide margin – collected more signatures than workers in other centres. Suffragists there were fortunate in having an ideal opponent, a man they could love to hate, in Henry Smith Fish, representative of the liquor trade in Dunedin city and in Parliament – the very stereotype of simplistic anti-suffragism and boorishness. As Maud Pember Reeves wrote to Hall, 'I regard it as an honour to the cause that men like Fish oppose it.' No wonder the five Dunedin newspapers covered a spectrum of opinion on the suffrage question, ranging from warm support in the *Evening Star* to total hostility in the *Otago Workman*.

In Dunedin, with its large working-class population, the WCTU first reached out to working-class women, some of them already organised in the New Zealand Tailoresses' Union by Harriet Morison. It was largely due to the support of working women, together with the excellent organisation of canvassers, that Dunedin women provided well over a third of the signatures on the 1891 petition, and a similar proportion for that of 1892. In April 1892 Nicol, Morison and Hatton organised the first Women's Franchise League, with Anna Stout as nominal president and Hatton as executive president. Morison urged women to support the suffrage campaign because they 'had to obey the same laws as men, had to pay the same taxes as men, and had a right to the same representation.' She travelled to Auckland, helping set up a league there, to which Amey Daldy was elected president. Smaller centres – Gore, Ashburton, Waimate, Feilding, Marton – quickly followed suit.

In centres where the WCTU was not actively involved in the suffrage campaign, the franchise leagues were especially important; in Wanganui the league was led by Margaret Bullock and Jessie Williamson. In Christchurch, where there was a substantial group of suffragists of both sexes clustered round the university, the Canterbury Women's Institute, established in September 1892, numbered among its many members Kate Sheppard, Ada Wells, Edith Searle Grossmann and Maud Pember Reeves; unlike the leagues, it accepted men as full members.

The success of the suffrage petitions spread panic in the

ranks of the liquor lobby, which responded by promoting anti-suffrage petitions in public houses in 1892. In Dunedin, where Henry Fish paid his anti-suffrage canvassers according to the number of signatures obtained, 5,000 names were said to have been collected; but Fish's credibility was severely dented when some were found to be fraudulent, and others those of women who had been misled into believing they were supporting women's suffrage. Late in 1892, in a significant flexing of political muscle, women ratepayer voters tipped the balance against Fish in the Dunedin mayoral election. 'Rejoice with us', wrote Marion Hatton to Hall, 'we have beaten Mr. Fish'.

In Parliament, neither the Liberal nor the opposition leaders would admit to being hostile to women's suffrage, but members held widely differing views about the roles women should play in society. Would the home-loving New Zealand wife be 'unsexed' by participation in politics, her grace and softness lost? Would her husband be less than a man to allow her to participate? Would the reform lead to unthinkable role reversals where wives made the speeches and husbands fried the chops? There were also calculations of political advantage. Some believed women were a radical force; others that they were conservative upholders of traditional values. While their adherence to the temperance cause was applauded in some quarters, it was feared in others. The suffrage issue cut across conventional lines of political allegiance.

There was steady support for the women's cause among Liberal backbenchers, but the attitude of ministers was less than straightforward. Ostensibly in favour of women's suffrage, some ministers quietly joined its opponents on two occasions in 1891. First, John Ballance introduced an Electoral Bill without provision for women's suffrage. When Hall's amendment incorporating it was obstructed by the liquor lobby, three ministers joined the obstruction. Then, after Hall's own Female Suffrage Bill passed its second reading with a majority of 25, the entire cabinet tried to delay its implementation until after the next election. Failing in this, they supported an amendment to allow women to sit in Parliament, in the confident expectation that this would be too much for the Legislative Council. In late September the bill was duly defeated there, 17 to 15.

The next year, when another Electoral Bill was introduced, allowing women the right to vote but not to sit in Parliament, it passed smoothly through the lower house. The Legislative Council, however, added an unexpected amendment. Women should enjoy 'electoral rights', that is, the right to a postal vote. The move reflected the opposition's attempt to appeal to country women, who were presumed to be a conservative force. It was too much, an advocate explained, to expect these women to travel several miles in order to vote, if the weather were inclement. The government would not accept the amendment, in spite of three conferences between the upper and lower houses. On the flimsy grounds that the secrecy of the ballot might be put at risk, the bill was defeated. 'That anyone ... could possibly think that to deprive 120,000 persons of the right to vote is preferable to running the risk of a few post masters opening sealed papers, passes our comprehension', wrote Kate Sheppard. It is evident, not only that the government negotiator, the shrewd and determined Richard Seddon, was glad of the opportunity to defeat the bill, but also that the government managed to force its backbenchers into line on the vote.

In 1893 both sides swung into action. Yet another petition, signed this time by nearly 32,000 women – between a fifth and a quarter of the adult female population – urged the adoption of measures to enable women to vote at the next general election, pointing out the 'grievous wrong' of denying women what had already been admitted by Parliament to be a just right. The timing of any change was perceived as crucial by the government. Even Ballance, an avowed friend of suffrage, feared for his party if women were to vote at the coming election. When in April Ballance's death brought Seddon to the premiership suffragists prepared for the worst. However, the government was publicly committed to women's suffrage. After Hall had introduced a further Women's Suffrage Bill, and in the course of its second reading rolled out the 300-yard long compilation of women's petitions, only three members voted against its introduction. It was a good omen, although it was noted that some members of the ministry absented themselves from the vote.

When the government's own Electoral Bill, with a clause on women's suffrage, passed through the lower house an important question was raised. Were Maori women included? Maori women are not recorded as having played a major role in the activities of the WCTU or the franchise leagues, and the issue of their enfranchisement had not been pressed by Maori members. But in 1892–93, at the same time as the European women's suffrage movement was reaching a climax, large sections of the Maori community had established their own parliament. In May 1893 Meri Te Tai Mangakahia presented to this parliament a motion to enable women to vote for and sit in it. She based her claim, which was well received, on the experience of Maori women in owning and managing their own land. Her case may have been strengthened by the fact that Maori women also conducted cases before the Native Land Court and had access to state education. When it was asked in the House of Representatives whether voting rights should be extended to Maori women, there was a roar of unanimous approval.

Seddon's opposition to the Electoral Bill was concentrated in the upper house, where 12 new councillors, appointed to facilitate government business, played a key role. Although the bill was an important government measure, it was not an issue of confidence and they had not been asked to support it. While the Legislative Council deliberated, therefore, both sides attempted to sway them. Enthusiastic suffrage meetings were held up and down the country. Wavering councillors received encouraging telegrams from the Auckland Franchise League and known supporters were given white camellias for their buttonholes. Liquor interests petitioned the Council to defer giving women a vote in licensing elections for five years. As the debates moved into the committee stage at the end of August there was unparalleled interest and excitement throughout the country. Attempted amendments to the bill – to defer the granting of suffrage to women until 1894, and to admit women to Parliament – failed to halt its progress, and so, by the slenderest of margins, did one directly opposing the principle of enfranchising women, and another reviving the electoral rights issue.

The vote on the third reading was marked by complex manoeuvres on the part of the ministry. It was evident that Council members were almost evenly divided. Seddon realised he needed one more vote to defeat the bill. He telegraphed one of the new councillors, who had left himself paired in favour of the measure, to change his vote. The ploy backfired. Angered by Seddon's action, two opposition councillors, who had favoured women's suffrage but only with the safeguard of electoral rights, changed sides and voted in favour. On 8 September the bill was passed 20 to 18. As the *New Zealand Herald* commented, 'it is hardly too much to say that the enfranchisement of the woman has been accomplished by her enemies'. On 11 September Seddon announced to a crowded House and gallery that the government would accept the bill.

Even at this stage the measure was not safe. Eighteen legislative councillors petitioned the new governor, Lord Glasgow, to withhold his consent. Suffragists responded by showering him with telegrams and requests to receive deputations. In Wellington the newly formed Anti-Women's Franchise League sent anti-suffrage members of Parliament red camellias, to contrast with the white ones worn by supporters. Anti-suffrage petitions were again opened for signature in public houses, often in return for free drinks, but once more many of the several thousand names collected were found to be bogus. On 19 September, finally, it was over. Seddon telegraphed Kate Sheppard to tell her the governor had signed the bill that gave New Zealand women the vote.

There was little time for campaigners to luxuriate in a sense of achievement. With the general election only 10 weeks away, the politically active of all persuasions joined in a

TARANAKI MUSEUM

*Election day 1893 in New Plymouth. Crowds gather near a polling booth in
Brougham Street where women and men are recording their votes.*

concerted bid to persuade women to register. Some were eager
to tell them how to vote. The Dunedin Women's Franchise
League, for example, as well as suggesting that women should
show gratitude to their friends in recent parliaments, drew
attention to the need for laws to protect themselves and their
children. Temperance workers were to the fore, as were
religious groups advocating Bible in schools or state aid to
private schools. Politicians naturally set out to woo the
women's vote.

The election itself passed off in a holiday atmosphere but,
it was noted with some relief, with due decorum. November
28, 1893 was a fine, bright day almost everywhere. Women
began to vote early and continued, with a break in the middle
of the day when 'dinner postponed politics', until tea-time.
Often the women of neighbouring families made up a party to
go to the polls, or neighbours took turns to look after each

ALEXANDER TURNBULL LIBRARY

*Women stand outside a rural polling booth at Tahakopa, South Otago,
having voted in their first election.*

other's children. 'All things', an interested male observer
assures us, 'were done in courtesy and order, without rude-
ness, hustling, or hysteria.' There was an impressive turn-out:
the 90,290 women who cast their votes made up about 85 per
cent of those registered.

The result of the 1893 election was a decisive victory for
the Liberals, to which the women's vote evidently contributed.
Commentators at the time claimed that women, especially
working-class women, merely voted the same way as their
husbands. However, their own reasons for voting Liberal,
whether for temperance reform, a better future for women
and children, or gratitude for enfranchisement, were strong.

Certainly women did not prove the solidly conservative force some had predicted. In some localities their influence could be recognised: the failure of Henry Smith Fish to retain his Dunedin seat was the most striking example. Friends of suffrage, such as George Grey and Robert Stout, were rewarded with handsome majorities.

In the three subsequent elections the number of women enrolled steadily increased to 185,944 by 1902; the proportion of those who voted remained about 75 per cent of those registered. Women's suffrage had 'gradually and, it would seem, permanently, entered into New Zealand life.' Suffragists in other democracies, most of whom would not achieve their political emancipation for another quarter-century, might well have been envious.

Why did New Zealand women succeed in gaining the vote so early? Kate Sheppard had no doubts: the reason was the 'vigorous and incessant agitation for the Franchise from one end of the colony to the other, never ceasing until womanhood suffrage had become an accomplished fact.' But other observers had a different view. The labour politician, W. P. Reeves, put it down almost entirely to political miscalculation. The extension of the franchise to women, he wrote in 1898 in his influential study, *The long white cloud – Ao Tea Roa*, was 'a curious example of a remarkable constitutional change carried by a Parliament at the election of which the question had scarcely been discussed.' The conviction of the opposition that its passage would bring down the government accounted for what he called the 'escape of the Bill in the Council.' Reeves reaffirmed this view at greater length in *State experiments in Australia and New Zealand* (1902), where he concluded that 'one fine morning of September 1893, the women of New Zealand woke up and found themselves enfranchised. The privilege was theirs – given freely and spontaneously, in the easiest and most unexpected manner in the world.' Reeves's claims did not go unchallenged. William Sidney Smith, who had been deeply involved with the movement throughout, provided a detailed account of the *Outlines of the women's franchise movement in New*

*Zealand* in 1905, but Reeves's opinions, set out in admired general works, became entrenched.

By 1908 the feminist writer Edith Searle Grossmann could take a longer view. In an article on 'The woman movement in New Zealand', Grossmann set women's enfranchisement in the context of a burgeoning feminism which worked to 'free women from artificial or barbaric restrictions' and 'give them fair opportunities and equal legal and political rights'. She attributed the early success of feminism in New Zealand to the fact that 'Many of the artificialities and conventionalities of an old civilisation were shaken off among the uncompromising realities of early colonial days.' A distinguished French political observer, André Siegfried, took a not dissimilar view; in 1914 in a chapter in *Democracy in New Zealand* entitled 'The feminist movement', he paid tribute to 'a group of men and women determined to realise the idea of woman suffrage' who 'managed to overcome the indifference of the many and the opposition of the few.'

A new wave of interest in women's suffrage in the 1970s reflected the wider perspective made possible by distance in time and the stirrings of second-wave feminism. Coral Lansbury, in 'The feminine frontier: women's suffrage and economic reality' published in *Meanjin Quarterly* in September 1972, explained the early grant of votes for women in New Zealand, Australia and some American states in terms of 'temporary political advantage which had little to do with a desire to equalize the roles of men and women in the community.' Also in 1972, in a full-length study, *Women's suffrage in New Zealand*, Patricia Grimshaw, judiciously balancing social, political and feminist factors, saw the achievement of women's suffrage in New Zealand as part of a general movement towards equality of the sexes. Raewyn Dalziel interpreted the New Zealand suffrage movement differently: in her 1977 article in the *New Zealand Journal of History*, 'The colonial helpmeet', she claimed that the vote was granted less in recognition of women's equality in society than of their special role within the home and family. While it may well have been easier to

HOCKEN LIBRARY

*Delegates to the first conference of the National Council of Women in Christchurch, 1896. Many former suffragists were prominent in what became known as the 'Women's Parliament'.*

achieve radical change in a new society without deeply entrenched conservative attitudes, the argument that women did not claim the franchise in an effort to undermine their traditional role in society is persuasive. They aimed, rather, to bring their special qualities to bear on public as well as private life.

What were the consequences of the early achievement of women's suffrage in New Zealand? Its impact on party politics appears to have been negligible. Seddon was glad to proclaim himself an advocate of the women's vote, and there was no backlash against it. In relation to legislation the issue is less clear. The National Council of Women of New Zealand, founded in 1896, gave suffragists the opportunity to apply pressure on the lawmakers and the laws. With Kate Sheppard as president and some former franchise leagues (Wanganui, Auckland, Gisborne) affiliated to the council as political leagues, the 'Women's Parliament', as the NCW was sometimes called, struck overseas observers by its radicalism and wide range of interests. The council pressed for the removal of all of women's political disabilities, repeal of the Contagious Diseases Act 1869 (which introduced compulsory medical examinations for women believed to be prostitutes), equal pay, equal divorce laws, economic independence for married women, and other reforms affecting women and children. In 1928 its president would list 44 acts on which she claimed the organised effort of women had had a decisive influence. Writing in 1930 the economic historian J. B. Condliffe agreed. In *New Zealand in the making* he stated categorically that the Divorce Act and Old-age Pensions Act of 1898, and the welfare measures that followed, were traceable to women's suffrage. More recent historians, however, have not been convinced, and a direct connection between the women's vote and subsequent welfare legislation has not yet been established.

In the afterglow of its passage, however, the beneficial effect of women's suffrage in New Zealand was much vaunted. Former opponents and supporters made surprisingly similar statements. Ten years after the franchise was granted Richard Seddon defended it with all the ardour of the convert: 'Who dares to propose that we should repeal the legislation that gave the franchise to the women of the colony?' he demanded, with rhetorical flourish and no apparent irony. 'In the legislation of which we boast, in the great social advancement we have made ... I say that women are behind it all'. In London, Maud Pember Reeves entered into vigorous debate in *The Times* on behalf of the women of New Zealand; and Anna Stout, in pamphlets and speeches, consistently lauded the legislation favourable to women that had resulted from the vote.

The example of New Zealand was important to suffragists overseas. The Australian experience was similar in many ways to that of New Zealand but complicated by the federal political structure. South Australian women were enfranchised in 1894 and those in Western Australia in 1899. In 1902 the federal government extended the suffrage to women; by late 1908 all Australian states had done so.

The British movement had far greater obstacles to face and used, in some cases, far more extreme tactics to counter them. In the early twentieth century traditional methods of promoting the cause, such as lobbying, writing pamphlets and holding processions, gave way to attacks on property, courting imprisonment to publicise the cause, even in 1913 the suicide of a woman under the hoofs of one of the King's horses on Derby day. The government responded harshly: imprisonment became routine, forced feeding countered hunger-striking, women made weak from the ordeal were released only to be detained again when their health was thought to be able to stand it. The First World War cut across this escalating conflict. At its conclusion in 1918 women over 30 were enfranchised, with full adult female suffrage being granted in 1928. A number of European states also gave women the vote in the years immediately following the war.

In the United States the road to the women's vote proved long. In 1890, after 20 years of thankless work, the two women's suffrage organisations merged, but the uniformly anti-suffrage stance of the southern states impeded progress. However, between 1910 and 1914 eight states enfranchised women. Another burst of suffrage activity at both state and national level in the latter stages of the First World War finally led to the passage and ratification of the Nineteenth Amendment to the American Constitution, giving women the vote, in 1919–20.

In the years after 1893 career opportunities for women in New Zealand expanded, but in politics women had a more restricted role. It had seemed a favourable omen that in the suffrage year itself Elizabeth Yates should have been elected mayor of Onehunga, the first woman mayor in the British Empire, but her term in office proved stormy and brief. An indirect influence on politics, through the NCW and through

*New Zealand supporters of the British women's suffrage campaign march in London
in 1910. Anna Stout stands left of centre in front of the banner.*

organisations concerned with specific issues of social reform,
was all that was open to New Zealand women for many years.
Women were not eligible to sit in the House of Representatives
until 1919 and none did so until 1933. No woman held a
cabinet post until 1947. The first Maori woman to be elected to
Parliament took her seat only in 1949. Countries which
enfranchised women long after New Zealand allowed them a
full role in political life much earlier. Despite constant pressure
from the NCW, New Zealand women were not accepted as
justices of the peace until 1926 or as jurors until 1942, and then
not on the same basis as men. Moreover, within a decade of the
vote being won the NCW had gone into recess and feminists
such as Margaret Sievwright and Jessie Mackay were expressing their disillusionment as the women's movement faltered.

    Nevertheless, women's role in society was advanced by the
suffrage movement, both through the experience it gave them
in organising together to achieve their rights, and in the

expanded sphere of public activity they claimed afterwards. The meaning of women's suffrage in New Zealand for those who participated in the struggle to attain it can be illustrated by the example of the three extraordinary Henderson sisters. All were committed to temperance; all spent their lives working for women.

The eldest, Christina, a secondary-school teacher and WCTU worker, was old enough to take a full part in the suffrage campaign and the NCW. Stella, trained as a lawyer, became one of the earliest women parliamentary reporters. After her marriage and move to Australia she made a name for herself as 'Vesta', a women's columnist on the Melbourne *Argus*, and later became one of the first women to represent Australia at the League of Nations. The youngest of the three, Elizabeth, as Elizabeth McCombs, was elected the first woman member of Parliament in New Zealand.

As a group the sisters are outstanding representatives of equal-rights feminism, but each one also worked for women's welfare, and saw her position of responsibility as a means to achieve this end. In 1938 Christina Henderson summed up what she believed New Zealand women had gained by the vote, enumerating those statutes enacted since 1893 which covered a broad range of social reforms, especially in relation to women and children. But she also made it clear that, for her, the real gain was not one of legislative achievement, but something more important: 'the mental and spiritual uplift resulting from the release of women from their age-long inferiority complex.' Her words encapsulate the spirit of the whole women's suffrage movement in New Zealand, to which they also make a fitting tribute.

*Dorothy Page*

Brookes, B. *et al.*, eds. *Women in history.* Wellington, 1986

Bunkle, P. 'The origins of the women's movement in New Zealand: the Women's Christian Temperance Union, 1885–1895'. In *Women in New Zealand society.* Ed. P. Bunkle & B. Hughes. Auckland, 1980

Dalziel, R. 'The colonial helpmeet: women's role and the vote in nineteenth-century New Zealand'. *New Zealand Journal of History* 11, No 2 (1977): 112–123

Dreaver, K. R. 'Women's suffrage in Auckland, 1885–1893'. MA research essay, Auckland, 1985

Evans, R. J. *The feminists*. London, 1977

Grimshaw, P. 'Tasman sisters: lives of "the second sex" '. In *Tasman relations*. Ed. K. Sinclair. Auckland, 1987

Grimshaw, P. *Women's suffrage in New Zealand*. Auckland, 1972

Labrum, B. ' "For the better discharge of our duties": the women's movement in Wanganui, 1893–1903'. BA (Hons) research essay, Massey, 1986

Labrum, B. ' "For the better discharge of our duties": women's rights in Wanganui, 1893–1903'. *Women's Studies Journal* 6, No 1/2 (1990): 136–152

Patterson, J. L. 'Woman suffrage in Dunedin, 1890–1893'. BA (Hons) research essay, Otago, 1974

Turner, K. W. 'Henry Smith Fish and the opposition to the female franchise in Dunedin, 1890–1893'. BA (Hons) research essay, Otago, 1985

# SEQUENCE OF SUFFRAGE EVENTS

1869   Mary Ann Müller ('Femina') wrote *An appeal to the men of New Zealand*, advocating votes for women.

1871   Mary Colclough ('Polly Plum') gave her first public lecture on the rights of women, including their right to vote.

1874   J. C. Andrew in the House of Representatives (the elected house of Parliament) urged that women be enfranchised.

1878   Robert Stout proposed in his Electoral Bill that women rate-payers be eligible to vote for and be elected as members of the House of Representatives. The bill was discarded because of a disagreement unrelated to women's suffrage.

1879   The Qualification of Electors Bill, introduced by John Hall, proposed giving women property owners the vote, but parliamentarians who wanted all women without exception to be enfranchised joined with those who opposed the reform to defeat the bill.

1880   The Women's Franchise Bill, introduced by James Wallis, lapsed after the first reading.

1881   Another Women's Franchise Bill was introduced by Wallis but was withdrawn before the second reading.

1885   The New Zealand Women's Christian Temperance Union was established following the visit of American temperance campaigner Mary Leavitt; by February 1886 there were 15 branches.

1886  At its first annual convention in Wellington, presided over by Anne Ward, the WCTU resolved to work for women's suffrage.

1887  Kate Sheppard was appointed national superintendent of the franchise and legislation department of the WCTU.

Two petitions requesting the franchise were signed by some 350 women and presented to the House of Representatives.

A Women's Suffrage Bill to enfranchise women and give them the right to sit in Parliament was introduced by Julius Vogel. Although a majority of members of the House of Representatives voted for the bill, political manoeuvrings led to its withdrawal at the committee stage.

1888  Two petitions asking for the enfranchisement of women were signed by around 800 women and presented to the Legislative Council (the upper house of Parliament).

1889  The Tailoresses' Union of New Zealand was established in Dunedin; many of its members, including the vice president, Harriet Morison, were to be active in the suffrage campaign.

1890  A Women's Franchise Bill introduced by Hall late in the parliamentary session lapsed, in spite of majority support, because there was no time to consider it. Hall then moved an amendment to the Electoral Bill to provide for women's franchise but this was defeated, mainly because its supporters were absent from the House when the vote was taken.

1891  Eight petitions asking for the franchise were signed by over 9,000 women and together presented to the House of Representatives.

Kate Sheppard began editing a women's page in the temperance newspaper, the *Prohibitionist*, to promote women's suffrage.

Hall moved an amendment to the government's Electoral Bill

to allow for women's suffrage, but debate was obstructed by its opponents in the liquor lobby and a vote was not taken.

A Female Suffrage Bill introduced by Hall received majority support in the House of Representatives but was narrowly defeated in the Legislative Council. An amendment allowing women to sit in the House of Representatives, inserted by the opponents of suffrage, ensured that the more conservative legislative councillors would not accept the bill.

1892    The Women's Franchise League, a non-temperance organisation which aimed primarily to obtain the vote for women, was established first in Dunedin by Helen Nicol, Harriet Morison and Marion Hatton, and later elsewhere.

The Canterbury Women's Institute, which campaigned for women's issues and the franchise, was founded in Christchurch by Ada Wells and other feminists.

Six petitions requesting the extension of the franchise to women were signed by over 19,000 women and presented as a group to the House of Representatives.

The Electoral Bill, introduced by John Ballance, provided for the enfranchisement of all women and was passed by the House of Representatives and the Legislative Council. However, predictable controversy over an impractical postal vote amendment caused the abandonment of the bill.

1893    Thirteen petitions requesting that the franchise be conferred on women were signed by nearly 32,000 women, compiled, and presented to the House of Representatives.

Meri Te Tai Mangakahia addressed the Maori parliament to ask that Maori women be allowed to vote for and become members of that body, but the matter lapsed.

A Women's Suffrage Bill was introduced by Hall in June but withdrawn in October, because it was superseded by the Electoral Act.

An Electoral Bill containing provisions on women's suffrage was introduced by Richard Seddon in June. During debate, there was majority support for the enfranchisement of Maori as well as Pakeha women. The bill was passed by the Legislative Council on 8 September (after last-minute changes of allegiance), and consented to by the governor on 19 September. The Electoral Act 1893 gave all women in New Zealand the right to vote.

*Women voters going up to a polling booth on election day 1899 in Auckland.*

*Disappointed that after two elections women had not voted for prohibition,*
*in July 1897 Lily Atkinson (Kirk) wrote in the* White Ribbon: *'in the*
*three years of her political power woman has not yet attained to perfection in its*
*exercise, perhaps not advanced far beyond the point reached by men*
*after centuries of practice.'*

# ATKINSON, LILY MAY
## *1866-1921*

Lily May Kirk was born at Auckland, New Zealand, on 29 March 1866, the daughter of Sarah Jane Mattocks and her husband, Thomas Kirk, a surveyor. In early 1874 her family moved to Wellington where Thomas Kirk, by this time a botanist, took up a position as lecturer in natural sciences at Wellington College (then affiliated with the University of New Zealand). Lily was educated at the Greenwood sisters' Terrace School. At home, she acquired Baptist convictions and a commitment to social service. With her mother and sisters she taught English to Chinese immigrants and reading skills to factory girls. Although she was never to leave the colony she spoke French and German fluently and read widely.

Lily Kirk joined the Women's Christian Temperance Union shortly after its inception in New Zealand in 1885. She supported total abstinence, stating that the 'slight pleasure that indulgence brings to the respectable modest drinker is as a feather's weight against the load of woe that drink lays upon numbers of our fellow creatures'. Her involvement in the temperance movement went hand in hand with advocacy of women's suffrage.

Throughout her life Lily Kirk held a variety of offices within the WCTU: dominion recording secretary (1887-1901), president of the Wellington branch (1896), and dominion president (1901-6). She was a dominion vice president for a period after 1906 and became recording secretary again shortly before her death. As a member of the legal and parliamentary department of the WCTU she was frequently in the gallery of the House of Representatives, and her 'intimate acquaintance with parliamentary usage' was invaluable to the union. She gave briefs on all bills which affected women, children or trade in alcohol, maintaining that women must take an intelligent interest in politics before advocating vigorous action.

She had a firm belief in the ability of women to effect change, and held that in the home, the nursery and the social circle the influence of women was supreme: 'If her power to mould the minds of the young and the social customs of the adult ... were exerted ... constantly and strenuously ... women might, without for a moment leaving the private sphere to which some old-fashioned critics would confine her, effect a glorious and bloodless revolution, the like of which the world has never seen.'

During the WCTU campaign for women's suffrage, Lily Kirk addressed audiences throughout Wellington province. She was always a popular speaker – in the backblocks as well as the city – delighting her listeners as much by her 'bright and racy manner' as by her persuasive earnestness. She capitalised on the camaraderie which flourished in the union, addressing her audiences as 'beloved comrades' or 'sisters', and urging them on as 'crusaders', so that, as a West Coast secretary reported, 'The appearance on the platform of Miss Kirk ... was the signal for an outburst of hearty greeting.'

From 1894 Lily Kirk was on the executive committee of the New Zealand Alliance, a prohibition organisation, and from 1895 until 1921 she was a vice president. In that organisation she worked closely with a Wellington barrister, Arthur Richmond Atkinson, who was prominent in the New Zealand Alliance, the Forward movement and the campaign against Richard Seddon. Arthur described Lily when she was his betrothed as a 'prodigy of talent, public and private ... a beautiful platform speaker & as strong off the platform where so many good platform hands are weak'. They were married at the home of a Wellington friend on 11 May 1900 and moved into a house in Wadestown. The following day Lily Atkinson resumed the campaign trail. She fitted easily into the formidable Richmond–Atkinson clan, many of whose members were also involved with the WCTU or the alliance. Within that family she was known, affectionately, as 'the waterlily'.

Lily Atkinson's identity was not swallowed up in marriage; in fact she and Arthur regarded themselves as colleagues engaged in a crusade rather than simply as husband and wife. Their favourite term for each other was 'agitator'. When Lily once apologised to her husband for finding housekeeping burdensome, he wrote in reply: 'The year has been a glorious one but for your weariness from domestic drudgery. We must better that at once, or else go into lodgings.' There were two offspring from the marriage: a boy, Tom, born in 1902 who lived for a few days only, and a daughter, Janet, born in 1904.

As Lily Kirk she had been present at the convention of the National Council of Women of New Zealand held in Wellington in 1898. During the conference, she had moved an amendment seeking recognition of the money value of a woman's work as wife and mother. At the 1901 conference, as Lily Atkinson, she was elected a vice president, and at this and later conferences spoke up for the rights of illegitimate children, urging state provision for their maintenance and education. She also expressed concern that divorce laws discriminated against women.

Lily Atkinson belonged to the Plunket Society, the Kindergarten Schools Society and the New Zealand Society for the Protection of Women and Children, of which she was president from 1903 to 1911 and vice president thereafter until her death. With her husband she promoted compulsory military training, and at the time of her death was a member of the Dominion Council of the National Defence League of New Zealand.

Lily Atkinson's robust and militant Christianity was as characteristic of her life as was her sense of humour and zest for campaigning. Asked on one occasion why she was on the platform and not at home darning stockings, she replied that she was 'fired with the true spirit of fair battle'.

After a brief illness, compounded by overwork, Lily Atkinson died suddenly at her Wadestown home on 19 July

1921, aged 55. In paying tribute to her, the editor of the *White Ribbon* proclaimed, 'Now that the torch has fallen from her nerveless hand, another must snatch it up, and waving it wide, send forth the ringing call to arms'.

*Frances Porter*

Grimshaw, P. *Women's suffrage in New Zealand.* Auckland, 1972

Obit. *Evening Post.* 20 July 1921

Obit. *White Ribbon* 27, No 314 (1921): 1–4

Porter, F. *Born to New Zealand.* Wellington, 1989

# BULLOCK, MARGARET
## *1845-1903*

Margaret Carson was born in Auckland, New Zealand, on 4 January 1845, the only daughter of four children born to Jane Kennedy and her husband, James Carson, a road maker. The Carsons had emigrated from Scotland; James Carson later worked as a carpenter and possibly a debt collector in Auckland.

Nothing is known of Margaret's early life. On 10 February 1869 at Auckland she married George Bullock, a warehouseman. The couple were to have five sons. On or about 17 March 1877, George Bullock died when the ship he was travelling on, the *May Queen*, was lost in a hurricane near Tonga. Margaret Bullock was left a widow with five children who were still 'mere babies'. Sometime in the late 1870s she took her family to Wanganui, where her eldest brother, Gilbert Carson, owned and edited the *Wanganui Chronicle*. Margaret Bullock joined him as a reporter, assistant editor and business associate for the next 10 years.

From about 1887 Margaret Bullock began to write short tales with local settings for English and New Zealand magazines and newspapers. 'Madge', as she often signed herself, gained a following throughout the colony. In 1894 she wrote her first and only novel, *Utu: a story of love, hate, and revenge*, under the pseudonym Tua-o-rangi. Based on her own research and set during the late eighteenth century, it was illustrated by Kennett Watkins, an Auckland artist who made a special study of Maori life and culture. *Utu* was dedicated to Sir George Grey, whom she admired for his 'intimate knowledge of the traditions ... of the Natives of New Zealand'. In writing the book, she wanted to 'preserve the memory of manners and

WANGANUI REGIONAL MUSEUM

*'Electoral Bill returned House for strangulation ostensibly amendment wire
Premier instantly'. Telegram from Margaret Bullock in Wellington
to Kate Sheppard in Christchurch when the Electoral Bill was
under threat in September 1893.*

customs now obsolete, and fast fading from the recollection of even the Natives themselves.' It nevertheless became a 'sensational story of the "shilling shocker" type', written to sell to a mass audience, at the request of a publisher. Subsequently Bullock wrote tourist handbooks for the government, publishing guides to Wanganui and Rotorua in 1897 and Taupo in 1899.

Margaret Bullock had an interest in painting, and was a working member of the Auckland Society of Arts between 1884 and 1886. In 1884 and 1885, as Maggie Bullock, she exhibited oil paintings including 'A Maori Hebe', 'Kawana Tiwhitorangi, a Wanganui chief' and 'Native girl'. However, like many women she devoted much of her spare time to voluntary work. Campaigning for women's rights and welfare activities kept her in the public eye in Wellington and Wanganui. While working for the *Chronicle*, Margaret Bullock became, after Laura Suisted, one of the first women parliamentary correspondents. This experience led her to believe that female suffrage would be the first step to ending discrimination against women. Her knowledge of the parliamentary system enabled her to smooth the passage of the Electoral Bill in 1893 when its success hung in the balance, by warning Kate Sheppard, the leader of the women's suffrage movement, of impending political obstruction.

In May 1893 Margaret Bullock established the Wanganui Women's Franchise League (known later as the Wanganui Women's Political League), which led the campaign for the vote in Wanganui. Once the vote was won, she visited every house in Wanganui, enrolling hundreds of women and explaining how their vote might count. She was vice president of the league until the inaugural president, Ellen Ballance, left for England, and was then president from 1893 until 1897. She served as a committee member from 1898 to 1900. She was also a central figure in the National Council of Women of New Zealand (NCW), holding the office of national vice president in 1900.

Margaret Bullock gave a number of papers at NCW meetings, including one on the 'burning question' of illegitimacy. She felt that it was a 'standing disgrace to civilisation and a satire on so-called Christianity.' Placing a legal disability on children was of no help in solving the problem. However, the need to remove 'women's disabilities' and to promote economic independence for women were Margaret Bullock's particular passions – evidently the result of her own experiences. In 1895, with two other league members, she met Premier Richard Seddon to discuss the removal of barriers to women's employment in the civil service and equal pay. Yet she did not support the temperance movement, and the feminist campaigns in Wanganui – in contrast with many other towns – did not involve the New Zealand Women's Christian Temperance Union.

Margaret Bullock became an official visitor to the female department of the Wanganui prison in 1896. She also worked for the elderly residents of Wanganui's Jubilee Home, publicising their appalling living conditions in trenchant letters to the local papers. Her feminist and welfare work often made her unpopular with local citizens. Yet while she pursued certain reforms, she did not question the fundamental structure of her society. As a member of a prominent Wanganui family, she and her children moved in élite circles, and she strongly defended the parliamentary system and the British Empire.

Personal adversity provided a counterpoint to Margaret Bullock's success in public life. Early widowhood was followed by continual ill health after she settled in Wanganui. In 1892 at Kai Iwi her son William died, aged 17, after falling into a threshing machine. By 1902 cancer forced her to withdraw from many of her activities. Despite an apparently successful operation, Margaret Bullock died on 17 June 1903, at her residence in Sydney Place, Wanganui.

Energetic and talented, Margaret Bullock was a pioneer in several respects. As a journalist and parliamentary correspondent she gained entrance into a predominantly male profession. She also played a pivotal role in the nineteenth century women's movement at both local and national levels.

In memory, she deserves to stand alongside better-known figures such as Kate Sheppard.

*Bronwyn Labrum*

Labrum, B. ' "For the better discharge of our duties": the women's movement in Wanganui, 1893-1903'. BA (Hons) research essay, Massey, 1986

Labrum, B. ' "For the better discharge of our duties": women's rights in Wanganui, 1893-1903'. *Women's Studies Journal* 6, No 1/2 (1990): 136-152

*Dolce Cabot considered the implications of women's franchise in an article, 'Do women need the suffrage?', published in the* Canterbury Times *on 21 September 1893. She concluded: 'It means a new educational power, for women will begin to study the wider national interests in which they are now to take an active part.'*

# CABOT, DOLCE ANN
## *1862-1943*

Dolce Ann Cabot was born at Christchurch, New Zealand, on 25 November 1862, the eldest daughter of Louisa Augusta Kunkel, whose father was a Prussian army officer, and her husband, Thomas Cabot, a farmer and language teacher from Jersey. After 1865 the family lived mainly on their farm at Otipua, near Timaru. Dolce was educated privately at first and is reputed to have read French and German by the age of 10. From late 1878 to December 1880 she attended Christchurch Girls' High School, then spent two years at the teacher training department of Christchurch Normal School before taking up a position at Timaru Main School, where she remained until 1891.

In 1887 Dolce Cabot began extramural study from Canterbury College, attending lectures in 1891 and 1892. She failed to complete her BA, but as a result of some trenchant articles on women's suffrage published in the *Canterbury Times* succeeded in gaining employment as editor of the 'Ladies' page' of that paper, a position she held from May 1894 until October 1907. Her appointment is said to have been the first of any woman to the staff of a New Zealand newspaper.

Dolce Cabot published some poetry and a few short stories; two poems were included in W. F. Alexander and A. E. Currie's anthology, *New Zealand verse* (1906). But she correctly identified journalism as her significant work. In contrast to the more common use of pseudonyms and anonymity, Cabot's weekly pages carried her own name, evidently signalling her determination to advance the cause of women. While she always included social and fashion notes, handy hints and syndicated material, her editorial purpose was

clearly educational: she reported women's successes and encouraged women to aim at professionalism – a quality much
praised in her own work – in all areas of their lives. Sensible
exercise and dress as a means to good health, proper training
for housewives and domestic workers, new career opportunities, and the practice and philosophy of education (with an
emphasis on the role and rights of female teachers) were
recurrent themes.

Equally important to the development of women, in
Cabot's eyes, were moral, humanitarian and artistic interests.
She recommended charity and common-sense Christianity;
denounced the sweated labour of Christchurch dressmakers;
deplored child marriage in India and the wearing of sealskin
coats; and organised collections for soldiers in South Africa. In
1894 she promoted the establishment of a women's orchestra,
and the following year, with Christina Henderson and others,
founded a club, known as The Idlers, which offered recitations
and music as a recreation for women of 'the brain-working
class'. She wrote knowledgeably about art.

Although Cabot's themes remained relatively constant
during her editorship, her political orientation changed. As an
ardent suffragist she had sympathetically reported meetings of
women's groups, and at a meeting of the Canterbury Women's
Institute in 1896 proposed a motion calling for the admission
of women to Parliament. But after the turn of the century she
displayed doubts about the extension of women's sphere, even
while she continued to advocate it. Typically for her time, her
ideological commitment to justice and equality for women was
always based on a belief in their inherent moral superiority
and the pre-eminence of their role as wives and mothers.

Dolce Cabot resigned from the *Canterbury Times* when she
married Andrew Duncan, a railway stationmaster, at Timaru
on 30 October 1907. Although she promised to continue as an
occasional correspondent for the paper, she appears to have
published little after this time. Seven step-children from her
husband's previous marriage, his career which entailed shifts
to Greymouth about 1910, Wellington in 1912 and Auckland in

1915, and his disinclination for public life may all have helped to curtail her literary activities. However, given her growing conservatism about working wives and her unswerving moral principles, Dolce Duncan most probably practised what Dolce Cabot had preached.

She continued to take a keen interest in education, especially that of women. In 1922 she helped launch the *Ladies' Mirror* in Auckland, contributing an article on 'The Auckland Women's Club' for the first issue, but published only two further articles in the magazine, on literary subjects. On her husband's retirement in 1922 the couple moved to Manurewa, and about 1928 returned to Christchurch, where Andrew died in 1935. Dolce Duncan died at Christchurch on 31 May 1943. The brevity of her obituaries is perhaps the clearest testimony to her withdrawal from public life in her later years: a few lines marked the career of a woman who, as a pioneer among journalists, had helped shape the opinions of a generation of Canterbury women.

*Helen Debenham*

'Miss Cabot, presentation by the staff'. *Canterbury Times.* 9 Oct. 1907

Thomson, C. H. 'New Zealand's women writers'. *Cassell's Magazine* (Feb. 1909): 307–311

AILSA CARADUS

*Elizabeth Caradus believed it was 'the gambling and drinking fraternity' who were 'afraid of the female voters.' She was applauded when she told a public meeting in Auckland that politicians who had voted against the abolition of the totalisator 'would either have to alter their views or go' once women had the vote.*

# CARADUS, ELIZABETH
## *1832-1912*

Elizabeth Russell was born in Falkirk, Stirlingshire, Scotland, on 26 April 1832, the eldest child of David Russell, a carpenter, and his wife, Elizabeth Adam. According to family information the Russell family lived in Perth, Perthshire. When Elizabeth was 10 years old the family emigrated to New Zealand on the *Jane Gifford*, arriving in Auckland on 9 October 1842.

The Russells lived in Mechanics Bay in two raupo huts, then in a wooden house. Elizabeth found employment with a cobbler in Queen Street, walking long distances to deliver boots. On 10 October 1848, at the age of 16, she married 25-year-old James Caradus, a prize-winning ropemaker. James commented that he had 'got a good wife who tries to make me and herself comfortable and has a desire to love God, which is a great treasure'. The couple were to have at least 15 children, seven of whom would die in infancy.

James Caradus set up a rope-walk, where hand-wound ropes were made, in Hobson Street, but did not prosper. After unsuccessfully seeking work as a carpenter he went to the goldfields of Otago, Ballarat in Australia, and Thames. However, he had no luck and the family was often 'pretty hard up'. While he was away, Elizabeth ran a small shop he had built in front of their house in Freemans Bay. In later years James and Elizabeth Caradus achieved a more settled existence, renting out small cottages James built in the Freemans Bay area. The shop stayed in the family until 1910.

Elizabeth and James Caradus shared a common interest in temperance and social work, and the poor area they lived in afforded many opportunities for such work. They attended the

Pitt Street Wesleyan Church and ran the Freemans Bay Mission in Union Street for many years. Elizabeth also became involved with the Ladies' Christian Association. She held mothers' meetings in Freemans Bay at which women sewed, talked and prayed. In 1885 the association became the third New Zealand branch of the YWCA. Elizabeth Caradus was a founding member, a vice president until 1900 and one of the first life members.

Her interests in women and temperance led Caradus to the first meetings of the Women's Christian Temperance Union, established in Auckland in 1885. She quickly became a key member of the WCTU and the Auckland branch of the Women's Franchise League, formed in 1892. Throughout the franchise campaign, and later, in the Auckland branch of the National Council of Women of New Zealand, Elizabeth Caradus was a leading figure. However, she rarely took a prominent office, perhaps because of financial restraints or business or family commitments. Caradus differed from most of the suffragist leaders in that she was of working-class origins and upbringing and had a large family to care for. Although she became treasurer of the WFL in 1893, she turned down the post of president of the Auckland branch of the WCTU. However, she frequently spoke publicly, moved resolutions and took part in deputations.

There is little evidence from which to assess the political views of Elizabeth Caradus. She did not appear to espouse a broad, equal-rights feminist platform, although she did attend the foundation meeting of the Tailoresses' Union of New Zealand in Auckland and was elected an honorary member, and she believed that women should be able to sit on charitable aid boards. Caradus seemed primarily concerned with moral reform and social work issues, including temperance, opposition to gambling, and repeal of the Contagious Diseases Act 1869. On this last topic, she took part in a deputation to the Auckland City Council where 'she spoke so forcible [sic] that one member of the Council acknowledged himself converted'. She took strong positions at meetings, on one occasion speaking 'with accustomed zeal' and on another giving an 'excellent and pithy' speech.

Elizabeth Caradus continued to attend WCTU and YWCA meetings in the first decade of the twentieth century. James Caradus died on 23 December 1906, and after a long illness Elizabeth died in Auckland on 5 November 1912. She was survived by seven children.

*Sandra Coney*

Caradus, A. *Courage and perseverance: the Russell–Caradus story.* Auckland, 1975

Coney, S. *Every girl.* Auckland, 1986

Dreaver, K. R. 'Women's suffrage in Auckland, 1885–1893'. MA research essay, Auckland, 1985

Macdonald, C. *et al.*, eds. *The book of New Zealand women.* Wellington, 1991

would in a body, as they came, "clear out," and why? because they have lived here now for nearly 20 years, and are as far off as when they arrived of seeing any practical legislation, and spirited enterprise inaugurated, to open up and benefit the country.—I am, &c.,
PIONEER.

Wainui, Wade, June 21, 1871.

## MRS. COLCLOUGH'S LECTURE.

### To the Editor of the HERALD.

SIR,—I did not wish my lecture published in either paper, because I intend to deliver it again, but I thank you for your long critique. I merely write to correct some errors. I am reported as saying that with me the matter of having a right to vote is a question of inclination and not of equity. What I did say was that it was a matter of equity and not of inclination. Then, again, Mr. Mill does not advocate obedience in wives, and I do. In the last place, I said that I did not think that women in any great numbers would ever concern themselves about politics, but that I think those who have proved good queens regent and self-helpful women demonstrate the capacity that is in women for government. There are several other inaccuracies, but these are the chief, and as they convey an idea of my sentiments at variance with my real opinion, I hope you will be good enough to insert this correction.—I am, &c.,
MARY A. COLCLOUGH.

## COROMANDEL. — THE BEAUTIFUL ROAD FROM THE WHARF TO KAPANGA.

### To the Editor of the HERALD.

On 26 July 1871 at Auckland, Mary Colclough delivered her first public lecture on women's rights. When she was mis-reported in the New Zealand Herald she responded with this letter.

# COLCLOUGH, MARY ANN
## *1836-1885*

Mary Ann Barnes was born in London, England, on 20 February 1836, the daughter of Susan Barnes and her husband, John Thomas Barnes, a carpenter. She arrived in New Zealand in 1859. At Onehunga on 9 May 1861, aged 25, she married Thomas Caesar Colclough, a farmer of 54 or 55, first in St Peter's Anglican Church then in the Catholic church. A daughter, Mary Louise, was born at Papatoetoe on 1 November 1862, and a son, William Caesar Sarsfield, was born at Otahuhu on 26 January 1864. Thomas Colclough died in the provincial hospital, Auckland, on 29 July 1867. As a well-qualified and experienced teacher Mary Colclough supported the family, running her own school for girls in Auckland from 1871 to 1872, and teaching at Tuakau from September 1872 and Kauaeranga from July 1873 on a salary of £200 a year. By late 1874 she had left for Melbourne, Australia.

To Aucklanders in the early 1870s Mary Colclough became a household name. As 'Polly Plum' she carried on an exhaustive public correspondence in the local press, taking on all comers. She gave public lectures in Auckland, Thames, Ngaruawahia and Hamilton – an extraordinary activity for a woman at that time. She advocated temperance and improved treatment of women prisoners and prostitutes, becoming involved in their practical rehabilitation. Above all, she championed women's rights.

Influenced by the writings of John Stuart Mill, Mary Colclough targeted the contemporary legal position of married women in New Zealand: they had no independent legal status, and no control over property or guardianship of their children. It was 'iniquitous', she argued, 'that in a Christian

country, anyone, male or female, should have it in their power
to wrong and oppress others, under the shelter of the law'. She
spoke from bitter personal experience: because of her own
husband's ruinous speculation with her earnings, bailiffs had
stripped the family residence down to bare floorboards. 'I was
the breadwinner,' she wrote, 'whilst he had all the bread-
winner's powers and privileges.'

She argued that women were entitled to education, careers
and the vote. In her opinion the role of wife and mother was
very important but it was absurd to educate girls purely for
domestic life. As single women, widows, or wives of improvi-
dent husbands, many would have to support themselves. Self-
reliance and self-help were the keys. There should be no legal
barrier to women rising as high in the world as their talents
would take them. Finally, justice demanded that women
should not be subject to laws they had no part in making.

Aucklanders, both men and women, reacted with outrage
or applause. Opponents ridiculed and patronised her, charged
her with impropriety of conduct, and condemned her on
biblical grounds. But many cheered. Her lectures drew enthusiastic audiences and women supporters were surprisingly
outspoken. All parties acknowledged her talent. The Reverend
Samuel Edger, a remarkable non-denominational minister
and father of Kate Edger, the colony's first woman university
graduate, was among her strongest advocates.

In late 1874, while in Melbourne, an even more radical
Mary Colclough attacked the institution of marriage itself and
challenged citizens to dispute with her on a public platform.
The Australian press was harsh and vociferous in its opposition to her ideas. Afterwards she returned to New Zealand, but
from then on disappeared from public view. At first she taught
in Auckland. She then moved to Canterbury, where from 1876
to 1878 she was headmistress of Rangiora Girls' School, and
in 1881, infant mistress at Papanui. She died in Picton on 7
March 1885, aged 49, a month after fracturing a leg and an
arm in an accident. She was survived by her two children.
Mary Colclough was a highly controversial public figure for a

few years only, but she jolted the people of Auckland by fundamentally challenging contemporary assumptions and values about woman's place in New Zealand society.

*Judith Malone*

Elphick, J. 'What's wrong with Emma? The feminist debate in colonial Auckland'. *New Zealand Journal of History* 9, No 2 (1975): 126–141

Evans, E. A. 'Polly Plum's battle for women'. *New Zealand Herald.* 17 Sept. 1975

McLintock, A. H. 'Colclough, Mary Ann, "Polly Plum" '. In *An encyclopaedia of New Zealand.* Ed. A. H. McLintock. Wellington, 1966

*Amey Daldy believed that those working for the suffrage cause would have to be 'wise as serpents, harmless as doves' if they were to 'win the day'.*

# DALDY, AMEY

*1829?–1920*

Amey Hamerton was born in Yarwell, Northamptonshire, England, and was baptised there on 14 June 1829. She was the daughter of Amey Bonfield and her husband, Charles Hamerton, a farmer. Her mother died when Amey was about 12, and her father remarried; little else is known of her early life. She arrived in Auckland, New Zealand, with her brother, John, on the *Caduceus* on 11 October 1860. On 13 January 1865 in Auckland she married William Henry Smith, a shoemaker; the couple did not have any children. They lived in Shortland Street; William Smith also owned properties in Gundry Street, and in Karangahape Road where Amey ran a 'ladies' seminary' and William a bootmaking business. On 2 April 1879 at the age of 62 William Smith died at Wairoa South (Clevedon), near Auckland. Captain William Crush Daldy was authorised by Amey Smith to identify the body. Less than a year later, on 17 March 1880, Amey Smith married William Daldy at Otahuhu, Auckland. William, a leading Auckland merchant and politician and previously a ship's captain, was a 64-year-old widower.

William Daldy's daughter, Frances Wrigley, had died in June 1879 survived by her husband, James Wrigley, and nine children. In April 1882 James also died, orphaning the eight remaining children. The Daldys placed them in a house next door to their home in Hepburn Street, Ponsonby, and employed a housekeeper. The children always thought of Amey Daldy as their grandmother.

Both Amey Daldy and her husband were staunch Congregationalists, and their religious beliefs helped shape their egalitarian views. In 1885 Amey Daldy became a foundation member of the Auckland branch of the New Zealand Women's Christian Temperance Union. She soon rose to a position of prominence in the organisation. In 1892 she represented the WCTU at a meeting held to revitalise the Auckland tailoresses' union.

On 1 June 1892 Amey Daldy spoke at a meeting held in Auckland to consider forming a branch of the Women's Franchise League. She claimed that although women wanted the vote, they did not wish to enter Parliament. However, she later explained her statement to Sir George Grey, whose views were more radical than her own, by saying that she 'did not want to frighten the public'. In contrast to Harriet Morison of the Dunedin tailoresses' union, who was opposed to men joining the organisation, Amey Daldy declared that 'she did not think the women would be able to do very much without them'.

Amey Daldy became president of the Auckland branch of the league. Driving around Auckland in a buggy with her grandchildren, she collected signatures for petitions on women's rights, often entering into spirited but amicable debates with local businessmen. She also chaired large gatherings in the City Hall theatre. A stern-looking woman with a high collar and hair swept up severely under a white lace bonnet, she became the subject of cartoons in the *New Zealand Graphic*.

Amey Daldy was supported in her political activities by her husband. At a lively meeting in July 1893, William Daldy spoke in favour of women's franchise. His statement that men were cowards for not extending the franchise to women excited one 'well-known identity', who leapt up and expostulated at length with the speaker. A policeman had to remove him. After another opponent, J. S. Duke, had forced his way onto the stage, Amey Daldy exclaimed that she was not surprised that women were refused the franchise 'if that was a specimen of the mankind of Auckland'. Women won enfranchisement that year, and immediately before the November 1893 election she urged every woman to record her vote: 'Let not babies, the wash-tub, or even dinners prevent the women going.' She arranged for women to care for children at each booth while their mothers voted.

In April 1896 Amey Daldy represented the Auckland branch of the Women's Political League at the first convention of the National Council of Women of New Zealand at Christchurch. Thereafter she attended the sessions each year, and in 1898 she became president of the NCW. Her feminist opinions matched those of other leaders in the organisation in their boldness for that period. In contrast to her public stance in 1892, at each session she moved that 'all disabilities be removed which at present hinder women from sitting as members in either House of the Legislature, or from being elected or appointed to any public office or position in the Colony'. Conditions of divorce should be made equal for men and women, she contended, and she also supported the repeal of the Contagious Diseases Act 1869. Speaking in favour of the widely unpopular NCW proposal that half of a husband's salary be paid directly to the wife to enable her to become economically independent, she argued, 'Is it right for any wife to be treated with less consideration than a paid housekeeper?' She also proposed that the law of coverture, which allowed men to treat their wives as chattels, be repealed.

Amey Daldy's Christian beliefs and sense of duty to others informed her opinions on other social issues. In her view the system of government in New Zealand should be reformed by introducing an elective executive, making changes to the Legislative Council, and establishing a board to appoint all public servants. The policy of the NCW was 'purification in administration of public affairs, and thence to the solution of great social problems', she stated. Together with Anna Stout, she opposed legislation restricting Asian immigration, arguing that it would be unjust to discriminate against other races. She supported the disarmament campaign and the principle of full employment. Independence of character ought to be developed, she believed, and she asserted that the true charity was to provide work. With regard to vice and crime, she thought that love and sympathy rather than fear and punishment should be used to reform the criminal. She proposed that it should become illegal to permit any person under 21 to enter a brothel, and that the age of protection of young persons be raised to 21.

Amey Daldy was contemptuous of the trivial concerns of ladies' columns in most newspapers and she urged women 'to educate themselves for the duties of life, and not for a round of frivolity'. Curiously, despite her democratic opinions, she opposed the extension of the municipal franchise to a residential qualification. Although she deplored the past conduct of local politicians, she believed that men who were used to dealing with large sums of money should manage municipal affairs.

The difficulties of travel and the poor health of her husband prevented Amey Daldy from attending the NCW sessions at Dunedin in 1900 and at Wanganui in 1901. She did, however, send a paper to Wanganui in which she expressed her opinion that girls should have equal advantages to boys in education, and that 'the choice of avocations ... be equally momentous whether the youth be girl or boy.' She reappeared in Napier in May 1902, holding the office of vice president, but was quiet compared to previous years. She supported motions for equal pay for equal work for men and women and for the introduction of moral instruction in state schools.

In 1903 Amey Daldy was unable to attend the September executive meeting of the declining NCW in New Plymouth because she was nursing her ailing, aged husband. She sent instead a handsome donation. William Crush Daldy died on 5 October 1903. He had consistently supported his wife and had always accompanied her to meetings and conventions. She was disconsolate after his death: 'few, if any, of our women know how much they owe to his influence in keeping me up to my duty, for I acknowledge that I did sometimes shrink from the odium of publicity and an unpopular movement. What I can do without him I do not know.'

In the euphoric aftermath of the South African war (1899–

1902) Amey Daldy attempted, unsuccessfully, to organise a meeting on peace and disarmament; but by this time support for reform was dwindling. In 1905 she wrote to leading suffragist Kate Sheppard: 'I have heard nothing of our women's movement for so long a time that I am wondering if the past has been all a dream and nothing more. . . . Why, oh why, do the women not rouse themselves from their love of ease and do something for the betterment of the race?'

Soon afterwards Amey Daldy suffered a stroke. Unable to speak or walk, she was confined to bed for 15 years until she died at Auckland aged 91 on 17 August 1920. She left legacies of £2,000 each to the New Zealand Congregational Ministers' Retiring Fund, the Salvation Army Rescue Fund, the Door of Hope Association, the Auckland YWCA, the NCW and the WCTU. Her bequest to the YWCA enabled the organisation to build a hostel in Auckland. A woman of radical views for her age and time, Amey Daldy campaigned fervently and fearlessly for women's rights and for social justice.

*Roberta Nicholls*

Coney, S. *Every girl.* Auckland, 1986
Grimshaw, P. *Women's suffrage in New Zealand.* Auckland, 1972
Holt, B. *et al. Women in council.* Wellington, 1980

*In September 1893 Learmonth Dalrymple telegraphed the governor, Lord Glasgow, urging him to assent to the bill which extended the franchise to women. Immediately it became law she organised canvassing in her district to place women's names on the electoral roll.*

# DALRYMPLE, LEARMONTH WHITE
## *1827?–1906*

Learmonth White Dalrymple was born to William Dalrymple and his wife, Janet (Jessie) Taylor, and was baptised at Coupar Angus, Angus, Scotland, on 21 July 1827. Her name at baptism was Larmonth Whyte Dalrymple. William Dalrymple was a prosperous merchant in ironmongery and agricultural products. Although his daughter would later complain of the inadequacy of her schooling, especially in mathematics, and express her hopeless yearning for 'mental culture', her education was not neglected. She attended Madras College in St Andrews, and later travelled in Europe, where she learned to speak fluent French. However, Learmonth Dalrymple was not entirely free to pursue her inclination for study. Her mother died in 1840 and as the eldest of eight surviving children she took over the considerable task of caring for the family.

In 1853 she set out with her father, two sisters and a brother for New Zealand. The family spent two months at Dunedin while their storm damaged vessel, *Rajah*, was under repair, and then travelled on to their destination, Wellington. However, they decided to return to Otago and by 1857 they had settled on a farm at Kaihiku, South Otago, where Learmonth Dalrymple kept house for the family and helped establish the first Sunday school in the district.

When the Otago Boys' High School opened in 1863, a leader in the *Otago Daily Times*, probably by Julius Vogel, urged a 'companion institution' for girls. This set Learmonth Dalrymple on a seven-year-long campaign, waged with discreet persistence, for girls' secondary education in Otago. She first appealed to her neighbour and friend, Major J. L. C. Richardson, speaker of the provincial council, initiating a fruitful collaboration in the cause of female education. Richardson advised her to 'go into town and get up a Ladies' memorial to the Council'. Meanwhile he himself moved a resolution there urging the submission of a scheme for girls' education to the next session. This resolution was unanimously affirmed. The 'Ladies' memorial' was less successful. It pointed out how 'inadequate and inefficient' were the existing facilities for girls' education and proposed setting up a school especially for 'the middle and wealthier classes of the colony'. Although moderately worded, its reception was mixed and the council took no action on it. This first phase of the agitation culminated in a public meeting of about 30 women in November 1865. It opened with due decorum, but a series of interruptions, from press reporters, a breathless woman with news of a buggy accident, and a German band outside the windows, turned it into pure farce and caused its abandonment.

The campaign revived before the end of the decade, largely owing to the quiet perseverance of Learmonth Dalrymple, now living nearer to Dunedin, at Port Chalmers. As well as fostering an informal group of Dunedin women supporters, she wrote some 700 or 800 letters to British educationalists and local politicians. In 1868, at her instigation, Provincial Treasurer Julius Vogel tried unsuccessfully to put £1,000 on the estimates, for a girls' school. She then looked higher, winning over Superintendent James Macandrew, who called for proposals from the education board, and in 1869 set up an education commission chaired by the Reverend D. M. Stuart and including nine provincial council members.

Learmonth Dalrymple promptly formed a ladies' committee, and as its secretary she wrote to the commission specifying what kind of school was desirable. Her ideas were based on advice from Frances Buss, famous principal of North London Collegiate School for Girls. She recommended that girls' education should 'in all essential points ... be assimilated to that of boys'. The proposed school should have adequate buildings, be in the charge of 'a lady, un-married, or a widow, of attested talents and acquirements' and 'embrace all the branches included in the term "thorough English Education,"' as well as physical training. Fees should be £10 per annum, the school day should open with prayer, and there should be accommodation for boarders. The commission incorporated these suggestions in their report to the provincial council. A principal, Margaret Gordon Burn, was appointed and Otago Girls' High School opened on 6 February 1871 with 78 pupils, the number rising to 130 by the end of the year. The first public high school for girls in the southern hemisphere was securely established.

Learmonth Dalrymple then transferred her lobbying skills to an allied cause, admission of women to the planned University of Otago. Again she received the support of Richardson, who was chancellor when the university opened in July 1871. With her helpers she organised yet another petition, this time to the university council, for 'admittance of ladies'. Many of the 149 signatories were wives of prominent men and their names lent weight to the appeal. On 8 August 1871 the council voted unanimously to admit women, the first university in Australasia to do so.

Besides maintaining her interest in the girls' high school, to which she donated prizes, and the university, where she founded a women's scholarship, Learmonth Dalrymple worked for the kindergarten movement, publishing a pamphlet on the Froebel method of early childhood education.

In 1881 she moved with her father to Feilding, to be near her brother John Dalrymple. She remained there after her father's death the next year. In this period her interests centred on the new Women's Christian Temperance Union and its campaign for women's franchise; she joined the Wellington branch and was later president of a branch at Feilding. Towards the end of her life her health and memory began to fail and she returned to Dunedin. She died at Ashburn Hall, Dunedin, on 26 August 1906, but was buried at Palmerston North.

A woman of great determination, Learmonth Dalrymple

was also a woman of her time. Her sense of decorum demanded not only that she keep in the background of Richardson and her male allies, but also that she find a married woman to preside over any public meeting or committee she organised. She claimed to disapprove of any education which made women 'clever, restless and unfeminine' and led to the 'wild cry for . . . an impossible equality with man'. Nevertheless she opened the way for New Zealand women to seek this equality by entering careers hitherto closed to them. From 1886 a steady stream of women, trained at Otago Girls' High School, would graduate from the University of Otago. Nor was her influence confined to Otago. The girls' high school quickly became a model for those in other centres, and the New Zealand university colleges followed Otago in admitting women. In time the principle that women should receive degrees on equal terms with men was accepted. Learmonth Dalrymple's efforts laid the foundations of higher public education for women in New Zealand.

*Dorothy Page*

Gardner, W. J. *Colonial cap and gown*. Christchurch, 1979

Trotter, M. *William and Isabella Trotter*. Invercargill, 1983

Wallis, E. *A most rare vision: Otago Girls' High School, the first one hundred years*. Dunedin, 1972

[Wallis, E.] 'Learmonth Dalrymple'. In *A new earth: pioneer women of New Zealand*. Ed. K. Glasgow. Tauranga, 1975

# EDGER, KATE MILLIGAN
*1857-1935*

Kate Milligan Edger, the first woman in New Zealand to gain a university degree, was born on 6 January 1857 at Abingdon, Berkshire, England, the daughter of Louisa Harwood and her husband, the Reverend Samuel Edger, a Baptist minister and graduate of the University of London. Kate was the fourth living child in a family of four girls and one boy. This intelligent and musical family, who pronounced their surname 'Edgar', produced a number of individuals who distinguished themselves.

After Samuel Edger was appointed as minister to accompany emigrants to the Albertland settlement north of Auckland, the family sailed for New Zealand on the *Matilda Wattenbach*, leaving London on 31 May 1862. Later the Edgers moved to Auckland, where Samuel held non-sectarian services for many years.

Kate received most of her early education from her father, probably in company with her sisters. Both she and her younger sister Lilian were able students, but there was no secondary teaching for girls in Auckland. With her father's support Kate obtained permission from Farquhar Macrae, the headmaster, to study with the top class of boys in Auckland College and Grammar School. As the only girl in the class she was required to enter with downcast eyes, and seldom spoke to her classmates who, she later said, treated her courteously. Although Auckland University College would not open until 1883, the school was affiliated to the University of New Zealand, thereby providing her with the opportunity to work towards a degree.

In applying for a scholarship, Kate wrote to the chancellor

NELSON COLLEGE FOR GIRLS

*Kate Edger (Evans) publicly advocated women's franchise on the grounds that those who were 'to be affected by the laws must have a voice in making the laws.'*

of the university: 'I am a candidate for one of the Mathematical Scholarships of the University of New Zealand to be awarded at the Examination in May. My age is within the specified limits, and I have received instruction privately and also in Latin and Mathematics at the Auckland College Evening Classes.' She mentioned her age and qualifications but not her gender. The senate, which wanted both to avoid controversy and to increase student numbers, accepted her application without comment and she was then able to proceed to her degree course.

On 11 July 1877 Kate Edger was awarded the degree of bachelor of arts, the first woman in the British Empire to earn this degree. At her graduation in Auckland, which was attended by a crowd of nearly a thousand, the bishop of Auckland, W. G. Cowie, presented her with a white camellia, which he said represented 'unpretending excellence'. No better symbol for Kate Edger could have been chosen.

A few months after graduation she became first assistant at Christchurch Girls' High School, where Helen Connon, the first woman in New Zealand to gain the degree of master of arts, joined the staff the following year. While teaching, Kate Edger studied at Canterbury College for an MA, which she obtained in 1882. Her sister Lilian graduated MA with her.

Shortly afterwards Edger was appointed the first principal of Nelson College for Girls at a salary of £350 per annum, with board and lodging provided. She had to begin by deciding what equipment was needed for the school, which opened in February 1883. In the early days she was responsible for the general supervision of the boarders, a task which she seems to have found uncongenial and of which she was relieved in 1885. Her teaching programme was a very full one. She taught English grammar, composition and literature, physical science, Latin, mathematics, singing, geography and even club swinging. In addition she prepared some of the senior girls for university scholarships and carried out the administrative work of a principal. She was a gifted teacher who commanded the respect and affection of her pupils.

Although she had to carry on her work in unsatisfactory buildings, Kate Edger and her excellent staff, which for two years included her sister Lilian, worked extremely hard. She committed herself to establishing a school which could provide a first-class education for girls. When the council of governors could not afford to provide equipment for the school, she paid for it herself; she also paid for an extra scholarship to allow one girl to stay on longer at school. During this time in Nelson Kate and Lilian Edger edited two volumes of their father's lectures and writings.

At Auckland on 6 January 1890 (her 33rd birthday) Kate Edger married the Welsh Congregational minister, William Albert Evans, whom she had met the previous September. She informed the council of governors that she intended to continue working after the marriage, but in fact resigned two months later, presumably because she was pregnant with the first of her three sons. Her seven hard-working years as the first principal had been of immense value to the school in its formative years.

While living in Nelson she occasionally preached in her husband's church. He resigned in 1893 and the family moved to Wellington, where William became involved in the Forward movement, which combined adult education with charitable and philanthropic work. Since this was unpaid Kate became the bread-winner. Working from the family home in Mount Victoria she conducted a private school at secondary level for girls in the morning and coached adult pupils in the evening. She also found time to help in the Forward movement by giving occasional lectures and working among the poor of the city.

Her husband's appointment to the charge of Newtown Congregational Church in 1904 relieved her of some of the financial strain. It is not clear when she gave up the school but she continued coaching pupils until 1912. Her work examining for university entrance, which she had begun in 1891, continued at intervals until 1929, and during the First World War she worked for two years in the Department of Education. She always supported her husband in his work, teaching in the Sunday school, helping with the choir and learning – when over 50 – to play the organ.

Before New Zealand women gained the vote in 1893 Kate Evans presided over suffrage meetings and made speeches on behalf of the cause. She was president and vice president of the Wellington branch of the New Zealand Society for the Protection of Women and Children from 1897 until at least 1928. Until the early 1930s she was active in the Women's Christian Temperance Union of New Zealand: in the Nelson branch, as dominion recording secretary from 1916 to 1920 and 1922 to 1930, as president of the Miramar branch, and as associate editor for some years of the union's journal, the *White Ribbon*. She was a member of the Newtown school committee and was dominion secretary of the League of Nations Union of New Zealand, as well as secretary of its Wellington branch. At the golden jubilee of Canterbury College in 1923 she headed the woman graduates' section of the procession through the streets of Christchurch.

Kate Evans was not strongly feminist in outlook. In 1923 she wrote an article, 'The first girl graduates', which asked and answered the question of whether the higher education of women had justified itself. 'It is too soon yet', she wrote, 'for a complete answer to be given to this question, but thousands of university women are proving by their lives that it has not unfitted them for home-making, the noblest sphere of women's work.' In fact, although devoted to her husband, as he was to her, and to her sons, Kate Evans did not excel at housekeeping and sensibly employed help, giving her energies to teaching and voluntary work.

After her husband's death on 6 November 1921, Kate Evans continued to live in Wellington until 1932, when she moved to live with her second son, Elwyn, and his family in Dunedin. Although now frail, she travelled from Dunedin to attend the golden jubilee of Nelson College for Girls in Easter 1933 and told the assembly that it was the power of thought that had enabled her to make the journey. Until her last days she continued to address the wrappers for the *White Ribbon*.

Shortly before her death in Dunedin on 6 May 1935, she was awarded the King's Silver Jubilee Medal. Obituary articles recognised her importance as the first woman in the country to graduate, and in doing so to demonstrate beyond argument women's intellectual capacity. The significance of her degree and her work in the development of two major schools for girls establish her place as one of the leading pioneers for women's education in the country. Although small and slightly built, with a quiet, reserved manner, she showed throughout her life remarkable stamina and a determination to achieve her ends.

*Beryl Hughes*

Obit. *Auckland Star.* 8 May 1935

Voller, L. C. *Sentinel at the gates.* Nelson, 1982

# FULTON, CATHERINE HENRIETTA ELLIOT
## *1829–1919*

Catherine Henrietta Elliot Valpy was born on 19 December 1829, the third daughter of William Henry Valpy of the East India Company and his wife, Caroline Jeffreys. There is some confusion about her birthplace: it may have been Cheltenham, Gloucestershire, or Reading, Berkshire. She was educated mostly in England, by an uncle, the Reverend Peter French. At this time she was also influenced by another uncle, the Reverend Charles Jeffreys, who had strong evangelical beliefs. Her formal education was supplemented during 1845 and 1846 when the Valpy family toured Europe. The young Catherine's impressions of Italy were chronicled in painstaking detail in the earliest of her surviving diaries.

In January 1849 the Valpys, with five of their six children, arrived at Otago on the *Ajax*. On 22 September 1852 Catherine Valpy married James Fulton, at a joint wedding with her sister Juliet Valpy and William Mackworth. The ceremony took place at her parents' home, The Forbury, Dunedin. James Fulton held land in West Taieri, called initially Ravensbourne, and later Ravenscliffe, to distinguish it from the West Harbour suburb of Dunedin. Except for brief sojourns elsewhere, Catherine Fulton lived there for the rest of her life.

On arrival in Dunedin Catherine Fulton had been a member of the most prominent family of Anglicans in the Otago community. The ease with which she took her place in Presbyterian Dunedin may be explained by her familiarity with evangelical views. Not long after her marriage she and James Fulton joined the Presbyterian ministers' sustentation fund at West Taieri, where they took leading places in the

OTAGO EARLY SETTLERS MUSEUM

*In 1890, as the debate on women's suffrage intensified, Catherine Fulton pointed out that many women paid rates or property taxes, and argued that taxation without representation was tyranny.*

congregation. Weekly church services were held for many years in their house, and Catherine Fulton started and taught a weekly Sunday school and Bible class which continued to meet under her guidance for nearly 70 years. She was also baptised at the Hanover Street Baptist Church in 1868. The baptism did not change her religious adherence, but she experienced a state of grace.

Throughout her marriage Catherine Fulton kept daily diaries in which she attempted to record dispassionately the fine detail of her daily life. The surviving diaries, which cover the years from 1857 to 1919, reveal the trials and successes of pioneering life. From them we learn that the bread often did not rise; that Dolly Richmond was a most 'aesthetic young lady & Isa Blackett also too-too'; and that household help was occasionally insolent. Catherine Fulton records her involvement in numerous organisations. She also describes the talents of her sisters and brother and their families, her husband and her eight children.

While facility with pencil or paintbrush was common to many members of her family, Catherine Fulton was best known for her musical talent and taste. She regularly played whatever instrument was available at the local church services, and the story of how her piano came to grief in the Taieri River before reaching its new home is recorded in her autobiography as well as by her brother-in-law, F. C. Fulton, one of the party responsible for its loss.

Catherine Fulton's beliefs led her to become involved in various social, political and religious movements. She organised and chaired the Tract Depot for a number of years, and started the Band of Hope Coffee Rooms which she helped run with her sisters Ellen Jeffreys and Arabella Valpy. She was a constant attender at Dorcas and mothers' meetings, and was deeply concerned for the moral and social welfare of the young people in the Otago Benevolent Institution and the Otago Industrial School, which she and her husband supported.

In May 1885 Catherine Fulton helped found the Dunedin branch of the Women's Christian Temperance Union and was its first president. She was the dominion president from 1889 to 1892, when she resigned because a constitutional amendment with which she agreed was not passed. The amendment stated that members of the WCTU could be eligible for election as officers only if they accepted the biblical doctrine of the Atonement.

Catherine Fulton was also an ardent advocate of women's suffrage and in 1891 records her and her friends' bitter disappointment when John Hall's Female Suffrage Bill was lost in the Legislative Council by two votes. She expressed her exasperation with Henry Fish, a Dunedin MHR, whose opposition to the bill was, in her words, 'outrageous and insulting'. She was also infuriated with Walter Carncross, MHR for Taieri, who introduced what she called a 'mischievous' amendment. He moved that women should be eligible to be members of the House of Representatives. As he had intended, the motion enraged members of the Legislative Council and the bill was defeated. Two years later in November 1893 when Catherine Fulton voted for the first time, Carncross did not get her vote, nor that of the many women she drove to the Outram polling station on election day.

Catherine Fulton's political sympathies were echoed by her husband, who, as a prominent politician, supported women's suffrage and the temperance cause. Her unmarried daughter, Caroline Fulton, was also a tireless worker for temperance, women's franchise and evangelical church organisations. After James Fulton died in 1891, Catherine Fulton managed the stud farm at Ravenscliffe, and continued to pursue her many interests until her own death on 6 May 1919.

*Rosemary Entwisle*

Federated Farmers of New Zealand, Women's Division. *Brave days: pioneer women of New Zealand.* Dunedin, 1939

Fulton, C. H. E. Autobiography, 1915. MS 846. DUHO

Fulton, C. H. E. Diaries, 1845–1846, 1857–1917. MS. DUHO

Fulton, F. C. 'First of the Fultons'. MS. Private ownership

# GROSSMANN, EDITH SEARLE

*1863-1931*

Edith Howitt Searle was born on 8 September 1863 at Beechworth, Victoria, Australia, the fourth child and third daughter of Mary Ann Beeby and her husband, George Smales Searle, a newspaper editor. The family came to New Zealand in 1878. Edith attended Invercargill Grammar School, and in 1879 Christchurch Girls' High School, where she became head girl. The principal, Helen Connon, took a particular interest in Edith, introducing her to Professor John Macmillan Brown of Canterbury College and persuading her to remain at school so she could gain entry to university. Helen Connon was to be not only a teacher and friend of Edith Searle but also a model: a woman who had achieved prominence in her career as a teacher and who believed in the importance of education for women.

In 1880 Edith Searle entered Canterbury College on a university junior scholarship. She later commented that there were then only three other girls at the college, but by the end of her course there were about 100 female students. She was awarded a senior scholarship in 1882, graduated BA in 1884 and received an MA with first-class honours in Latin and English and third-class honours in political science in 1885. A brilliant student, she won a number of prizes and was a member of the debating society. Among the topics she debated were the higher education of women and the Married Women's Property Bill of 1884. Macmillan Brown described her as 'an indefatigable worker . . . [whose] talents placed her amongst the foremost.'

After graduating Edith Searle taught at Wellington Girls' High School until 1890. On 23 December that year, at

*ANNALS OF NEW ZEALAND LITERATURE*

*'Why should anyone suppose the act of voting will change nature?' asked Edith Grossmann in an article, 'Woman suffrage', published in the* Canterbury Times *on 1 October 1891. 'Womanhood is something so distinct from manhood it leaves its own impress on all its acts and circumstances.'*

Wainuiomata, she married Joseph Penfound Grossmann, who had been a fellow student at Canterbury College. The couple lived for a time in Christchurch where Joseph taught at Christchurch Boys' High School. Their only child, Arthur Searle, was born in Christchurch on 5 December 1894. In 1897 Edith tutored university classes in Wellington. She subsequently lived in Auckland, and spent 10 years apart from her husband in England and Europe. Joseph Grossmann was twice convicted of fraud in 1898 and was sentenced to two years in prison. He later became professor of history and economics at Auckland University College, until being dismissed from his professorship in 1932.

Edith Searle Grossmann (the name by which she is best known as a writer) published four novels between 1890 and 1910: *Angela; a messenger* (1890); *In revolt* (1893); *A knight of the Holy Ghost* (1907), republished the following year as *Hermione; a knight of the Holy Ghost*; and *The heart of the bush* (1910). Grossmann was involved in the suffrage movement in the 1890s, and her fiction was part of that struggle for the vote and for equal rights for women within marriage. Her understanding of the women's movement was consistent with that of other nineteenth century feminists, who argued that women's superior moral fibre and their place within the family gave them a special role in public and political life. The women's movement was 'breaking down worn-out conventions,' she wrote; its members 'were throwing open one door after another to women; they were raising the white flag of a purer morality; they were lifting up the fallen, trampled victims of social wickedness'. She also wrote of the need to 'raise the idea of marriage. The union is marriage, and the union is the source of the new race', and described the lives of New Zealand women as a 'combination of feminism and home-life'.

Her feminist views are most clearly expressed in the novels *In revolt* and *Hermione*, which focus on the character Hermione Carlisle. Here she examines women's education, the role of women in marriage and the restrictive laws surrounding marriage, the place of religion in the subjection of women, and possible solutions to the inequities women faced. The idea that women had access to a higher morality than men was explored in Grossmann's first novel, *Angela*, in which a young woman is wrongfully accused of involvement with a married man. Angela joins the Salvation Army and serves the downtrodden in Wellington and Sydney. In all three novels the purity and morality of the female protagonists is destroyed by the wickedness of a cruel, patriarchal world: Angela is murdered by a man she has attempted to save from execution, and Hermione commits suicide because her marriage confines her to a relationship with a drunken and abusive husband who takes property which has been willed to her.

In her fourth novel, *The heart of the bush*, Grossmann seeks solutions to the issues raised in the previous three, and looks particularly at the role of women and marriage in a colonial society. The unlikely marriage between the English-educated Adelaide Borlase and the manager of her father's Canterbury station, Dennis MacDiarmid, threatens to go wrong because both are deluded about the other's expectations of the relationship. The two are made to confront their erroneous ideas about each other when Adelaide nearly dies in childbirth. The result is a compromise in which she gives up her ideas of 'civilising' Dennis, and he realises that her happiness does not require the riches of European culture.

In her own life Edith Searle Grossmann achieved more than the women's movement aimed for. In addition to her novels, from 1897 to 1918 she wrote as a free-lance journalist for British and New Zealand newspapers and journals. Her subjects included Maori education, the conservation of old buildings, the development of parks within cities, literary criticism, theatre and fiction. She published a life of Helen Macmillan Brown (Helen Connon) in 1905. She was a founding member of the Lyceum Club in London, and of the Canterbury Women's Institute in Christchurch in 1892. Edith Searle Grossmann died on 27 February 1931, at home in St Heliers Bay, Auckland, and was buried at Hillsborough.

*Heather Roberts*

Cvitanovich, L. *Breaking the silence.* Palmerston North, 1985

Morgan, A. J. 'Edith Searle Grossmann and the subjection of women'. MA research essay, Auckland, 1976

Obit. *Press.* 7 March 1931

Roberts, H. *Where did she come from?* Wellington, 1989

*Speaking to women in Oamaru after the failure of the 1891 Female Suffrage Bill,
Marion Hatton remained optimistic: 'There are, however, some of us women who,
after a casual study of political history, have just sense enough left to know that
there cannot possibly be any such thing as finality in politics.'*

# HATTON, MARION
## *1835–1905*

Mary Ann (known as Marion) Hanover was born in Preston, Somersetshire, England, probably on 8 September 1835, the daughter of Elizabeth Stenner and her husband, Robert Hanover, a licensed victualler. She was working as a milliner when she married Joseph Hatton, an accountant, at Bath on 7 October 1855. Before and after her marriage she engaged in Sunday-school work and the temperance campaign conducted by the Band of Hope Union. The Hattons went to Amsterdam to further the temperance cause by establishing the first lodge of the Good Templars there.

It is not known when Marion and Joseph Hatton arrived in New Zealand, but Marion first publicly identified herself with the campaign for the enfranchisement of women when she chaired a pro-suffrage meeting in Dunedin on 12 April 1892. The behaviour and verbal attacks of the mayoral candidate, MHR and head of the liquor lobby, H. S. Fish, goaded the Dunedin suffragists to remove the prohibition issue from the suffrage campaign. The Women's Franchise League was established a fortnight later, and Hatton became president. She was backed by her husband, who, as secretary of the local prohibition league, had already made public its resolution to the government requesting that women's enfranchisement be incorporated in the Electoral Bill. Marion Hatton's work in the church and the temperance movement gave her a common ground with many suffragists, but because the WFL had made winning the franchise its sole concern, the movement had become attractive to a broader spectrum of women.

Both Marion Hatton and Harriet Morison, then secretary of the Tailoresses' Union of New Zealand in Dunedin, stressed that the key to the league's campaign was organisation. Collecting signatures for the suffrage petitions circulated each year from 1891 to 1893 was seen as crucial for putting pressure on the government to enact legislation. Hatton explained the league's strategy: 'we shall want all the help we can command, and all classes and conditions of women should be made available . . . we shall hope to be in a position to map out the whole of the city and suburbs for our canvassers'. Dunedin was the largest city in New Zealand in the 1890s, and therefore an important centre in which to make the petition successful.

With Helen Nicol, the WFL's secretary, Marion Hatton also introduced the league's tactics to other centres. The pair travelled to townships in South Canterbury, Otago and Southland to speak at suffrage meetings. Despite having a soft voice, Hatton was the league's principal speaker. On these visits she emphasised the importance of a thorough canvass for the petitions. The league's efforts were rewarded. Many women outside the temperance movement, especially those unionised by Morison, supported the petitions and Otago returned by far the largest number of signatures.

Marion Hatton made women's suffrage the key issue of the mayoral election in Dunedin in 1892. Of H. S. Fish she stated: 'we are pledged as a League to vote down the man who had done the worst he knows to injure our cause in the House of Representatives, and who has insulted the women of this colony, as no other man ever dared to do before.' An exchange between the two took place in the newspaper, with Marion Hatton exhorting those women with the municipal vote to favour 'the candidate most likely to defeat Mr Fish.' Fish was unsuccessful, and later admitted that the women had been shrewd tacticians in distributing a circular the day before the election when he had no time to reply. The vote of women property owners was recognised as being decisive and 'a perfect answer' to those who were sceptical of women's interest in and commitment to politics.

After New Zealand women had won the right to vote in parliamentary elections, Marion Hatton continued to develop her ideas on women's rights. While many of her contemporaries saw prohibition as the most important issue, her main aspiration was to redress the inequality of women before the law. Her particular concern was that women be given the same pay as men for performing the same tasks equally well. She also helped to initiate the National Council of Women of New Zealand, and in 1896 attended the inaugural conference in Christchurch.

Hatton remained president of the Women's Franchise League, which provoked controversy in 1895 by publishing a political manifesto. Its aims were 'the consolidation of the political rights already won, the extension of the privileges opened up by our present political position, and the furtherance of all those claims by which we seek to place woman in her rightful position amongst men.' There was also a practical aspect to the WFL's beliefs. During the winter of 1895 it opened and maintained soup kitchens for the unemployed of Dunedin.

Marion Hatton suffered from heart disease, and her hard work for charitable projects may have adversely affected her health. She died in Dunedin on 6 June 1905, survived by her husband, five sons and a daughter.

*Jean Garner*

Grimshaw, P. *Women's suffrage in New Zealand*. Auckland, 1972
Obit. *Otago Witness*. 14 June 1905

CANTERBURY MUSEUM

*In 1918 Christina Henderson urged members of the*
*Women's Christian Temperance Union to lobby*
*for the right of women to stand for Parliament:*
*'Members of Parliament must be made to understand*
*that we mean business. Every Union should see to it*
*that the local Member of Parliament knows*
*that his vote is being watched.'*

# HENDERSON, CHRISTINA KIRK
*1861–1953*

Christina Kirk Henderson was born, according to family information, on 15 August 1861 at Emerald Hill, Melbourne, Australia. She was the second of nine children of Alice Connolly and her husband, Daniel Henderson. Her mother had been a governess at the time of her marriage; her father was variously a trader, storekeeper, grocer, flax-miller and clerk as he moved from Victoria to Tasmania, and then, in 1863 or 1864, to Auckland, New Zealand. A brief sojourn in Tauranga in the late 1860s was followed by periods in Kaiapoi and Ashburton before the family finally settled in Christchurch around 1882.

The Henderson children were brought up in an old-fashioned Presbyterian way, 'on porridge and the Shorter Catechism.' They were all voracious readers; Christina possessed an excellent library and always gave presents of books to her nieces and nephews. She attended school in Auckland, Kaiapoi and Ashburton. By December 1878 she was a pupil-teacher at Ashburton School, attending teacher training classes before and after school and on Saturday mornings. She then won a scholarship to complete her training at the Christchurch Normal School. In 1881 she passed the examination for a class D certificate and was briefly relieving headmistress at the Normal School. From 1883 to 1885 she taught at Springston School, at the same time enrolling for part-time study at Canterbury College. She graduated BA from the University of New Zealand in 1891.

Daniel Henderson's death in 1886 left his widow struggling to bring up the youngest members of a large family on a low income. Christina Henderson helped to support the family for many years, a burden which increased when her older sister Alice began work as a missionary in 1896. In 1886 she obtained a position at Christchurch Girls' High School, where she remained until her retirement from teaching in 1912. She became first assistant in 1889 and was acting lady principal for a time in 1898, but apparently the board of governors considered her too radical to be appointed permanently. A highly respected though stern teacher, Henderson taught Latin and English, established the school magazine and was first president of the debating club. An active cyclist and walker (she tramped the Milford Track in 1900), she also assisted with annual sports days.

Her upbringing and straitened circumstances left Christina Henderson with a serious nature, strong religious beliefs and socialist sympathies. Her principles were fostered by her membership of a small socialist club in Christchurch during the 1880s. She saw capitalism as cruel and unjust, especially to 'the weak, disorganised masses' of women workers. Her own position as a female teacher, earning only half the pay of men doing the same job, confirmed her belief in equal pay for equal work. 'It is quite true that a woman manages to live on less than a man because her wants are fewer, but it is equally true that her wants are fewer because her earnings are less', she wrote tartly. Henderson became the first president of the Association of Women Teachers, founded in 1901 to secure a better status and remuneration for women teachers.

She had an abiding concern for the welfare of women and children. In the early 1890s she joined the women's franchise campaign and the Canterbury Liberal Association, and in 1898 the Canterbury Children's Aid Society. To these causes Henderson would bring formidable energy, a clear, logical mind, superb writing and organisational skills, and a vigorous approach based on exhaustive knowledge. Henderson also became a member of the National Council of Women of New Zealand, and was secretary from 1902 to 1905. It was she who maintained contact with the International Council of Women after the New Zealand body foundered, and she was one of three women who were responsible in September 1916 for reviving the organisation. Henderson became secretary again in 1919, but resigned for health reasons in 1922; possibly the conservatism of the new NCW did not appeal to her. She also served as secretary (1917-19) and then president (1919-24) of the Christchurch branch. She fought for the right of women to serve as police, members of Parliament, jurors and justices of the peace; she herself was appointed a justice of the peace on 23 February 1928.

Christina Henderson's deepest enthusiasm was reserved for the prohibition campaign. She was conscious of 'the futility of advocating other reforms, when so few women could be economically independent and when drunkenness brought misery and poverty to so many homes.' An early member of the Christchurch Prohibition League, she was honorary secretary from about 1901 until 1913. In 1912 she edited the *Reformer*, a prohibition magazine. From that year, freed from all domestic responsibilities except gardening, which she loved, social reform became her life. 'I hope that everyone will think only of the work – the worker doesn't count', she wrote.

Christina Henderson's long association with the Women's Christian Temperance Union of New Zealand began in 1913 when she was elected corresponding secretary and legal and parliamentary superintendent. Until 1938 she was responsible for scrutinising all legislation affecting women and children, a task involving countless letters, petitions, submissions and deputations. Henderson was a strong advocate of work with the young and was also actively involved in patriotic work during the First World War. She was president of the Christchurch branch of the union from 1926 until 1946, and continued to attend meetings until the year of her death.

Alice Henderson's mission work led Christina to take an active role in the Presbyterian Women's Missionary Union of New Zealand. She served as secretary (1917-20) and president (1930-32), but her main contribution was her editorship, from 1923 until 1946, of *Harvest Field*, the union's magazine. Christina brought 'sympathy and encouragement' to Alice's

years of missionary endeavour, visiting her twice and supporting her financially. The two sisters shared a missionary union
house at Sumner in the last years of their lives. Christina,
whose mind remained clear to the last, died aged 92 in the
Public Hospital, Christchurch, on 27 September 1953. She
had never married.

Christina Henderson was 'singularly undemonstrative',
and often seemed unloving to her family despite her passionate
affection for them. She had, however, a keen and subtle sense
of humour, and her pungent wit was often interspersed with
trenchant sarcasm. 'She gave of her best to any cause that she
considered was for the betterment of the community and was
not deterred by difficulties', but she expected others to meet
her own high standards.

*Patricia A. Sargison*

Allan, S. M. 'Nine of us'. MS. CMU
'Miss Henderson: an appreciation'. *Harvest Field* No 408 (1946): viii–x
Obit. *Outlook.* 6 Oct. 1953
Obit. *Press.* 29 Sept. 1953
Obit. *White Ribbon* 25, No 9 (1953): 4

# MACKAY, JESSIE
## *1864–1938*

Jessie Mackay was born on 15 December 1864 at Double Hill station, above the Rakaia Gorge in Canterbury, New Zealand. She was the eldest child of Elizabeth Ormiston and her husband, Robert Mackay, a shepherd who managed successively the Double Hill, Raincliff and Opuha Gorge stations in Canterbury. Jessie was educated at home until 1879, when, at the age of 14, she went to Christchurch to train as a teacher at the Christchurch Normal School. She taught at Kakahu Bush School from 1887 to 1890 and at Ashwick Flat in 1893–94. In 1898 she moved to Dunedin where she began working as a journalist, but returned to Christchurch in 1902 to take up a position at Inveresk School.

When illness forced her to abandon the teaching profession in 1904, Jessie Mackay developed her career as a journalist. She had been writing a fortnightly column for the *Otago Witness* from 1898, and only returned to teaching, reluctantly, for financial reasons. She was to continue to write for the *Otago Witness* for 30 years. In 1906 she was appointed 'lady editor' of the *Canterbury Times*. When that paper closed in 1917 she turned to free-lance writing, contributing to the *White Ribbon*, the journal of the Women's Christian Temperance Union of New Zealand, and to British feminist journals such as *Jus Suffragii*, *Votes for Women* and the *Common Cause*, and writing for the weekly *Time & Tide* as New Zealand correspondent.

From 1911 Jessie Mackay shared a cottage at New Brighton, and later a larger home in the Christchurch suburb of Cashmere, with her younger sister, Georgina, who like Jessie never married. Their mother had died in 1897 and the following year Robert Mackay's business partner was declared

'Is't an army treading nearer? is it swarming bees that hum?
'Tis the women at the polling-booth: Emancipation's come.'
From 'The sitter on the rail' by Jessie Mackay, published with other poems in 1891.

bankrupt, leaving the family in financial difficulty. Jessie supported herself and her sister financially by her journalism, but she was equally occupied with political activity and writing poetry. She was involved in the suffrage movement in Christchurch in the 1880s and 1890s as a member of the WCTU, and is said to have collected names for one of the petitions seeking women's franchise. Through her journalism she campaigned for prohibition and penal reform, against vivisection, and for a number of feminist causes including the need for women in Parliament, better pay for women, and the recruitment of women into the police force. A pamphlet published in 1928, entitled *The girl of the drift*, discussed the social and moral responsibilities of women. Jessie Mackay was active in the National Council of Women of New Zealand from its inception and was one of three women who initiated its revival after 1916.

Just as strong as her feminism was her belief in home rule for Scotland and Ireland. Her parents had brought with them to New Zealand a wealth of Scottish culture and their children's early education was imbued with the myths, stories and legends of Scotland. In late 1921 Jessie Mackay left New Zealand on a trip to England, Ireland, Scotland and the Continent and in January 1922 attended the Irish Race Congress in Paris as a New Zealand representative of the Society for Self-Determination for Ireland.

Although this was her only visit to Great Britain, Jessie Mackay's affinities with Scotland in particular were as strong as those of someone who had been born there, and as a poet she is best known for her ballads based on Scottish legends. Her first volume of poetry, *The spirit of the rangatira*, appeared in 1889 when she was 25. Over the next 20 years she published three more volumes: *The sitter on the rail* (1891), *From the Maori sea* (1908) and *Land of the morning* (1909). The demands of making a living meant that she could not write as much as she may have wished, however, and it was another 17 years before she produced *The bride of the rivers* (1926). Her last volume of poetry, *Vigil*, appeared in 1935.

A number of Jessie Mackay's ballads have strong women as their focus. Her recognition of oppression and affinity with the oppressed are also evident in poems such as 'Cry of Armenia', and in a number of others which have a Maori theme. At a time when many people believed that the Maori were a dying race, Jessie Mackay saw that Maori culture had value, and that the so-called 'degeneration' of the Maori was the fault of European activities and not the result of some intrinsic weakness of the race. These beliefs are expressed most clearly in 'The charge of Parihaka', 'Departure of the Timaru volunteers for Parihaka' and 'Henare Taratoa', in which the New Zealand wars are seen to have been caused by Pakeha greed and violence. Mackay also used the ballad form to retell a number of Maori myths, including 'Rangi and Papa', 'Rona in the moon' and 'The noosing of the Sun-God'. Her best-known ballad, however, is 'The burial of Sir John McKenzie', which was published in the 1908 volume *From the Maori sea*. McKenzie, a Scottish immigrant and farmer like Mackay's own parents, became minister of lands in the Liberal government in the 1890s. His battles for reform of land tenure, which curtailed the power of large landholders and allowed small farmers to acquire land, appealed to Jessie Mackay's sense of justice.

Her passionate belief in social justice was balanced by a keen sense of humour. The early books of poetry contain a number of lighthearted yet perceptive pieces, such as 'Lament of the mateless stocking', a poem written in mock-heroic form in which the stocking left behind mourns the loss of its partner, and 'The old bachelor's lament'. Occasionally she used this sharp wit against those she saw as her opponents; in 'The sitter on the rail' she chastised those who refused to take sides on issues such as women's suffrage.

Jessie Mackay was connected with a wide range of literary people in both New Zealand and Australia. She corresponded with A. G. Stephens, the editor of 'The red page', the literary page of the Sydney-based *Bulletin*, in which a number of her poems were published, and with Australian writer and literary critic Nettie Palmer, who with her husband, Vance Palmer, was a major influence in Australian literary life particularly in the 1920s and 1930s. She counted among her close friends the writers Blanche Baughan (who also lived in Canterbury) and Eileen Duggan. In 1897 she presented a handwritten manuscript of over 100 poems to Edward Tregear, himself a poet and at that time head of the Department of Labour. A number of these poems were subsequently published in *Land of the morning*. She also knew the novelists Edith Searle Grossmann and G. B. Lancaster, to whom, along with Baughan and Stephens, she dedicated *Land of the morning*.

In 1934, on the occasion of her 70th birthday, Jessie Mackay was presented with a testimonial signed by writers, friends and admirers from New Zealand and elsewhere, as 'a demonstration of appreciation and affection'. The journalist and novelist Alan Mulgan wrote to the minister of finance, Walter Nash, in 1936 asking that pensions be awarded to Jessie Mackay and James Cowan in recognition of their contribution to New Zealand letters. Of Jessie Mackay he wrote: 'In addition to being a poet who has written some of our best lyrics, she has been a crusader all her life'. Pensions of £100 a year were granted. By this time Jessie Mackay was ageing and frail; but she was still writing, and still caring passionately about those causes to which she had devoted her life. Her last volume of poetry was published only three years before her death, at Christchurch, on 23 August 1938.

In the year of her death the New Zealand centre of the writers' organisation PEN established the Jessie Mackay Memorial Prize for verse. Her work was included in a number of anthologies of New Zealand poetry which were produced in her lifetime, and in the anthology edited by Robert Chapman and Jonathan Bennett in 1956. However, her exclusion from the 1960 *Penguin book of New Zealand verse*, edited by Allen Curnow, limited awareness of her contribution to New Zealand literature among later generations of readers. Mackay's place in the history of New Zealand poetry has been considerably under-recognised. As, in E. H. McCormick's assessment, the spiritual representative of a new generation of writers who emerged in the late nineteenth century, Jessie Mackay preceded the 'flowering' of New Zealand poetry in the 1920s and 1930s. Yet without her and others like her, who created an audience for it, that flowering would not have been possible. In her poem 'The gray company', from *Land of the morning*, Mackay described those who come 'Before the pioneers' – Huss who preceded Luther, Galileo who preceded Newton. The gray company do not know the companionship that the pioneers know: 'But the gray, gray company / Stood every man alone'; they experience 'scorning', 'jeering' and 'strife', and they pave the way for the pioneers. It is an apt description of Jessie Mackay's own place in the history of New Zealand poetry.

Jessie Mackay saw herself first and foremost as a poet. She cared about her literary reputation, and it is that reputation by which she has been judged in succeeding years. But an assessment of her life and work must place her creative writing in the context of the political activity and journalism to which she also devoted her life.

Like other women writers of her time, such as Robin Hyde, Jane Mander and Edith Searle Grossmann, Jessie Mackay had to earn her living to support herself and her relatives and tried to write in the spaces in between. Earning a living was in itself hard enough in a society where this was not an accepted pattern for women. She wrote to A. G. Stephens in 1903: 'When ruin overtook us four years ago, I had to take on a double sort of life – half woman's, half man's work. It is hard for even the most sympathetic man to understand how hard it is for a woman to obtain the conditions a man writer commands as a matter of course. Nobody's fault, you know, just the pains of transition.' Added to this constraint on her time for writing was the political activity in which she immersed herself. To see her only as a poet, or only as a social activist, is also to fail to recognise the interaction between these aspects of her life. Jessie Mackay was not alone in seeing imaginative writing as a vehicle for persuading others to a cause. Her crusading spirit informed her poetry, and her poetry is a record of all the causes she held dear.

*Heather Roberts*

Mackay, J. Papers, 1902–1930. MS Papers 778/1. WTU
Macleod, N. F. H. *A voice on the wind.* Wellington, 1955

MRS W. MAREROA

*In her address to the Maori parliament in May 1893, Meri Te Tai Mangakahia
said: 'E whakamoemiti atu ana ahau . . . ko te take i motini atu ai ahau,
ki te Tumuaki Honore, me nga mema honore, kia mahia he ture e tenei whare kia
whakamana nga wahine, ki te pooti mema mo ratou ki te Paremata Maori.'
(I move this motion before the honourable leader and all honourable members so
that a law may emerge from this parliament allowing women to vote and
women to be accepted as members of the parliament.)*

# MANGAKAHIA, MERI TE TAI
## *1868–1920*

Meri Te Tai was of Ngati Te Reinga, Ngati Manawa and Te Kaitutae, three hapu of Te Rarawa. She is said to have been born on 22 May 1868, near Whakarapa (Panguru) on the Hokianga Harbour. She was the great-grandchild of the woman of mana, Nga-kahu-whero. Her father, Re Te Tai, was an influential chief of Te Rarawa in the Hokianga district in the 1890s and later; her mother was Hana Tera. Hana's marriage to Re Te Tai was her second; three children had been born of her first marriage, to a member of the Parore family. Meri was the eldest of the four children of Hana's second marriage.

Family tradition suggests that Meri Te Tai was well educated. She is said to have studied at St Mary's Convent in Auckland, and was an accomplished pianist. In the late 1880s or early 1890s she became the third wife of Hamiora Mangakahia, of Ngati Whanaunga and other Coromandel hapu. He was an assessor in the Native Land Court, and was working at Waimate North in 1887. He was also at the Bay of Islands in 1889, attending the meeting at which Te Kotahitanga, the Maori parliament movement, was formally initiated.

Hamiora and Meri built a homestead on his land at Whangapoua on the Coromandel Peninsula. During the following years Meri gave birth to four children: two sons, Mohi and Waipapa, and two daughters, Whangapoua Tangiora Edith and Mabel Te Aowhaitini. Mabel Mangakahia became a registered nurse and midwife, and is thought to have been the first Maori to gain the postgraduate diploma in public health nursing in 1939.

Hamiora Mangakahia was elected premier of the Kotahi-

tanga parliament in June 1892. In 1893 both he and Meri
attended the second session of the parliament at Waipatu in
Hawke's Bay. The women's suffrage movement had been
gaining strength from the 1880s, and it is likely that Meri had
knowledge of this. She may, like many Maori women, have
come into contact with the New Zealand Women's Christian
Temperance Union, which campaigned for women's suffrage.
On 18 May 1893 the Speaker of the lower house of the Kotahitanga parliament introduced a motion from Meri Mangakahia,
requesting that women be given the right to participate in the
selection of members. It was suggested that she come into the
house to explain her motion, and later that day she addressed
the parliament – the first woman recorded to have done so.

She requested not only that Maori women be given the
vote, but that they be eligible to sit in the Maori parliament,
thus going a step further than the contemporary aims of the
European suffrage movement. She argued on the grounds that
many Maori women owned and administered their own lands,
either because they had no male relatives or because the
women were more competent. She claimed that although
chiefs had appealed to Queen Victoria over Maori problems,
Maori women had received no advantage from these appeals,
and suggested that the Queen might more readily respond to
representations by women.

Meri was followed in the debate by Akenehi Tomoana,
wife of Henare Tomoana, the host at Waipatu. Akenehi suggested that discussion of the issue be postponed until the men
had 'achieved their goal' – until, she appears to have meant,
they had succeeded in achieving recognition for the Kotahitanga parliament. The matter then lapsed.

Little further is recorded of Meri Mangakahia's participation in the Kotahitanga movement, but she continued to be
active in Maori politics and welfare. An oil portrait painted
about this time, preserved by her family, shows a beautiful
young woman dressed in the height of European fashion. It is
likely that she was a member of one of the women's committees
of the Kotahitanga movement. These committees, early fore-

runners of the Maori Women's Welfare League, organised the activities of young people attending Kotahitanga meetings, and undertook massive catering. They also held meetings and debated political issues.

Meri and Hamiora Mangakahia spent most of their last years together at Whangapoua. When Hamiora died in June 1918, Meri became one of the two executors and trustees of his complicated estate. He left his property at Whangapoua to their four children, with the proviso that Meri had the right to live there and be maintained by them. She returned, however, to her own people and lands at Panguru, taking some of her children with her. According to family information she died of influenza on 10 October 1920, aged 52, and was buried at Pureirei cemetery, Lower Waihou, near her father.

*Angela Ballara*

Macdonald, C. *et al.*, eds. *The book of New Zealand women.* Wellington, 1991

*Harriet Morison insisted that not only women temperance campaigners but all thoughtful and intelligent women wanted the vote as an 'undoubted right – not as a privilege but as a right.'*

# MORISON, HARRIET RUSSELL
## *1862–1925*

Harriet Morison was born in Ireland, probably in June 1862 at Magherafelt, County Londonderry, the daughter of Margaret Clark and her husband, James Morison, a master tailor. Little is known about Harriet's early life. She travelled with her family to New Zealand in 1874, and became a tailoress; through her occupation she began a lifetime involvement in working women's concerns.

In Dunedin in 1889 Harriet Morison became the first vice president of the Tailoresses' Union of New Zealand. This was created after the sweating scandal of late 1888 and early 1889 exposed appalling working conditions for factory employees and home-workers in Dunedin. The union was the first organisation to represent female workers in New Zealand effectively. After John A. Millar stepped down as secretary in 1890, Harriet Morison took over the position, having carried out the secretary's duties for the previous six months.

For the next six years she was an important force within the tailoresses' union. Owing largely to her energy and commitment, the union raised wages and established industry standards for tailoresses throughout Otago. She also assisted workers in other provinces. In 1892 Harriet Morison spent seven months in Auckland organising northern tailoresses. She returned there many times, helping to ensure the survival of the union in Auckland. Maintaining contacts with tailoresses throughout New Zealand was important to Morison, as she believed that unity was vital to the tailoresses' cause. She was not, however, especially radical for her time, always advocating moderation and co-operation with employers in all union activities.

In 1890 Harriet Morison led an attempt to set up a domestic servants' association in Dunedin, with the dual purpose of providing a well-trained supply of servants to the ladies of Dunedin and raising the social status of domestics, giving them the 'dignity of skilled labour'. She felt that without training and skills, women would never improve their position in society.

Although known primarily as a trade unionist, Harriet Morison was active in many other areas. She led an unsuccessful attempt to set up a convalescent home for Dunedin clothing workers, and sat on a local committee to manage ambulance classes for women. She edited the 'Working woman's corner' in the *Globe* newspaper from January to March 1891. For 14 years she was an official visitor at Seacliff Lunatic Asylum just north of Dunedin. She was a lay preacher for the Bible Christian church and at another time served one term as chairwoman of her Unitarian church committee. Christianity was fundamental to her values: she believed that trade unions, as a means to achieve equality, were consistent with the teachings of Christ. Christian principles gave Morison's trade unionism a humanitarian aspect shared by many other moderate unionists of her time.

Harriet Morison also believed that women's right to vote was implicit in egalitarian Christian principles. The need to use the vote to counteract the evils of alcohol, and the injustice of ignoring half the adult population, were two other important arguments she used to back her demand for women's suffrage. She was a founding member of the Women's Franchise League in Dunedin, the first in New Zealand, which she formed in 1892 with Helen Nicol. Suffrage petitions circulated nation-wide in 1891 and 1892 owed many of their signatures to Harriet Morison, who helped to raise support among the working women of Dunedin. She was an important participant in a public campaign which helped prevent anti-suffragist H. S. Fish, member of the House of Representatives, from winning the 1892 mayoral election in Dunedin. She was also a member of the New Zealand Women's Christian Temperance

Union, an organisation which agitated for women's suffrage.

In 1896 Harriet Morison left the Dunedin tailoresses' union under a cloud. Inclement weather meant that two picnics she had planned in 1895 were a disaster. She organised a carnival to clear debts and raise further funds, but did not keep proper books and had the carnival bank account in her name. In 1896 members of the union's executive committee accused Morison, probably wrongly, of embezzling funds and dismissed her as secretary. She was never formally charged and the matter ended with her resignation from the union.

However, she continued to be an advocate for working women. Morison was appointed an inspector of factories for the South Island in April 1906, but the Labour Department quickly decided that she was an 'inappropriate choice'. She was accused of being 'rather inclined to go to extremes' and failing to conform to the 'steady, sure and tactful' departmental style. So many complaints were laid by factory managers that Morison was removed from her position, and in May 1908 she was placed in charge of a newly opened Women's Branch in Auckland, which was essentially a labour bureau for domestic servants.

In 1909 Morison was put on the department's retrenchment list but given a last-minute reprieve. She resented her demotion and also the directive in 1910 that she inspect factories for four hours per week accompanied by a male inspector. In 1913 and 1914 she was further upset by having to do at least two hours clerical work per day. In 1914 she appealed her classification, but was unsuccessful as senior officers were convinced she had exaggerated the extent of her duties. In 1917 they spurned requests from four Auckland women's societies and a number of individuals that a female inspector be employed, and that the appointee be Harriet Morison.

In February 1917 Harriet Morison was suspended on the grounds that she had falsified claims regarding the employment of servants (probably in an attempt to show her workload was incorrectly classified). An inquiry was held at which evidence supporting the case against her was produced. Just as she was about to be dismissed, amid strenuous protest from the Public Service Association, the prime minister intervened. Morison was reinstated but not subdued: in 1919 she applied for a salary increase. Finally, in 1921, Morison resigned from the public service when the Department of Labour closed the Women's Branches and made her and three other women redundant.

Harriet Morison died on 19 August 1925 at her home in New Lynn. She had never married. Morison left behind an important legacy, not only as a trade unionist, but also as a feminist. She provides an example of the strong connections between women workers and the battle for women's rights in New Zealand. Her belief that women had a duty to care for the morals of society as well as a right to be protected from its evils extended into her approach to trade unionism.

*Penelope Harper and Melanie Nolan*

Obit. *New Zealand Herald.* 20 Aug. 1925
Paul, J. T. *Our majority.* Rev. ed. Dunedin, 1939

# MÜLLER, MARY ANN
## *1819/20?–1901*

Mary Ann Wilson was born in London, England, probably in 1819 or 1820 and died at Blenheim, New Zealand, on 18 July 1901. Her father's name was James Wilson but nothing else is known about her early life. She married James Whitney Griffiths, a chemist, in London on 16 December 1841 and they had two children. In August 1849 she and her children left England on the *Pekin*. They arrived in Nelson in January 1850. Mary Griffiths was described on the ship's passenger list as a widow but it is almost certain her husband was still alive and that she had left him on account of his cruelty. On 5 December 1851 at Nelson, having ascertained Griffiths's death, she married Stephen Lunn Müller, a widowed doctor with four children, who had also come to New Zealand on the *Pekin*. In 1857 the family moved from Nelson to Blenheim, where Stephen Müller took up the position of resident magistrate.

Mary Müller had a keen sense of the legal and political disabilities of women, based on personal experience. Her first and greatest concern was that, on marriage, women lost all rights to own and control property. Her second concern was that women were not able to vote. In 1864 she met the English women's rights advocate, Maria Rye, who was visiting New Zealand, and from then on closely observed the course of the women's rights movement in Great Britain and the United States. She began, under the pen name 'Femina', to contribute articles on women's rights to the *Nelson Examiner*. Because of her husband's opposing views she had to work 'like a mole'. The editor of the *Nelson Examiner*, Charles Elliott, was a friend and relative by marriage of Mary Müller. He saw that the

*'Our women are brave and strong, with an amount of self-reliance, courage, and freedom from conventionalities eminently calculated to form a great nation. Give them scope.' From* An appeal to the men of New Zealand *written by Mary Ann Müller in 1869.*

articles were widely distributed and soon her influence extended well beyond Nelson.

In 1869 she wrote the first pamphlet on the woman's vote published in New Zealand, *An appeal to the men of New Zealand*. In it she argued that women should not be discriminated against in law or politics on grounds of their sex, that they had as just a claim to the vote as men, and that without political rights they could not make their full contribution to the progress of the nation. 'How long', she asked, 'are women to remain a wholly unrepresented body of the people?' She urged men to take the initiative in electoral reform and made a special plea to parliamentarians: 'Women's eyes turn in hope – nay trust – on some leading spirits who will not fail them.' In 1870 Mary Müller received a letter of congratulation from John Stuart Mill, to whom she had sent a copy of her pamphlet. Mill urged her to form a committee to work for the vote, but she was unable to act publicly. However, she subsequently met and influenced politicians, notably Alfred Saunders and William Fox.

Acts to protect the property of married women were passed in 1870 and 1884, and in 1893 women won the vote. Mary Müller witnessed these reforms with pleasure and in 1898 she wrote to leading suffragist Kate Sheppard: 'Old & failing, it is cheering to watch the efforts of the younger and abler women striving bravely to succeed in obtaining rights so long unjustly withheld'. In December 1898, seven and a half years after her husband's death, her identity as 'Femina' was finally revealed. She then became known, through the writings of Kate Sheppard, as New Zealand's pioneer suffragist.

*Raewyn Dalziel*

Grimshaw, P. *Women's suffrage in New Zealand*. Auckland, 1972

Harper, B. *Petticoat pioneers*. Book 3. Wellington, 1980

Sheppard, C. W. Papers, 1870–1916. MS. CMU

*In 1892, before the vote was won, Helen Nicol told a public gathering in Oamaru that 'if women had had a voice in electing members of Parliament, long ere now our fair colony would have had something to be proud of.'*

# NICOL, HELEN LYSTER

## *1854–1932*

Helen Lyster Nicol was born on 29 May 1854 in Edinburgh, Scotland, the sixth of 10 surviving children of Margaret Cairns Smith and her husband, David Nicol, head gardener at the Orphan Hospital in Edinburgh. When Helen was two years old, the Nicol family left Scotland on the *Strathmore* and arrived at Port Chalmers, New Zealand, in October 1856. They were Free Church settlers and strict Sabbatarians, and Helen remained a staunch church member all her life. Her father worked as a gardener for two years for W. H. Reynolds and James Macandrew. He prospered and bought 200 acres of rural land and part of a block in central Dunedin. All this property he bequeathed to his unmarried daughters, Helen and Lavinia, who inherited it when he died in 1890.

Helen Nicol taught in the ragged Sunday school, and this experience made her familiar with the poverty and desertion which many women and children endured. Convinced that drink was the fundamental cause of all social evil, she became a lifetime abstainer and prohibitionist. She joined a number of temperance organisations; at various times she was a member of a Band of Hope, the Juvenile Temple, the Independent Order of Good Templars, the Blue Ribbon Army and the New Zealand Women's Christian Temperance Union (WCTU). Particularly concerned with children, under the auspices of the WCTU she set up the Loyal Temperance Legion, which provided vocational training.

Helen Nicol's zeal for temperance led her to work for the enfranchisement of women. Her aim was for women to elect 'men of good moral character' who would enact prohibition, thereby restoring purity to the home. She argued in favour of women's rights and pointed out the ways in which women were disadvantaged by the law, stating, 'We do not want a seat in Parliament, but we do want a vote to put the right kind of men there.'

Helen Nicol pioneered the suffrage campaign in Dunedin. She wrote letters to the press and, as superintendent of the franchise department of the Dunedin branch of the WCTU, corresponded with other suffrage leaders, most notably Kate Sheppard and Sir John Hall. The women of Otago returned the highest number of signatures to each suffrage petition. Such work took its toll. Helen Nicol wrote of the weariness she experienced, and Harriet Morison, first vice president and later secretary of the Tailoresses' Union of New Zealand, emphasised that her friend had stood up for suffrage 'when to declare one's self a woman's franchist was to bring down on your devoted head the ridicule of most of your friends'.

The suffrage campaign in Dunedin was especially bitter because of the vigorous drink lobby led by H. S. Fish, the city's member in the House of Representatives, where he headed the opposition to women's enfranchisement. In 1892 Fish organised a counter-petition to the pro-suffrage petition then being circulated. Confusion was such that Helen Nicol started yet another petition to enable those women who had signed in error, believing that Fish's petition was pro-suffrage, to protest.

In response to Fish's 'hostile attacks' Harriet Morison, assisted by Helen Nicol and other women, founded the Women's Franchise League in Dunedin in 1892. Its sole aim was to win the vote. It reached out to those beyond the temperance lobby and built on Morison's work for the tailoresses' union, tapping the support of the large number of young women working in the clothing establishments in Dunedin. Helen Nicol and Marion Hatton, the league's Dunedin president, held public meetings in rural townships in Otago and Southland. One journalist described Nicol as very tall but with a light voice.

After the vote was won, Helen Nicol described herself as

'one who worked harder than any other woman in the South Island for the extension of the franchise to every woman'. She continued to campaign for temperance and was for a time involved with the National Council of Women of New Zealand. Although disappointed that prohibition had not become law, she wrote: 'I have never regretted spending the best years of my life in working to secure the enfranchisement of our New Zealand women, and I do feel that it has bettered the position of the workers'.

Increased domestic responsibilities curtailed Helen Nicol's public life from 1897. She and her sister, Lavinia, reared three nephews, one of whom spoke of Helen as being 'very, very kind.' Helen Nicol had 'no respect for the man or woman who neglects the sacred duties that make home happy'. In later life she welcomed the new opportunities that arose to promote the welfare of women and children. Her mother died in 1904 and Lavinia, who was also engaged in charitable work and writing to the paper, eventually married. Helen Nicol never married; she died in Dunedin on 22 November 1932.

*Jean Garner*

Grimshaw, P. *Women's suffrage in New Zealand*. Auckland, 1972
Obit. *Otago Daily Times*. 28 Nov. 1932

C. RATTRAY

*Lizzie Rattray was reported as saying at a meeting of the Women's Franchise League in Auckland: 'if every scoundrel had a right to vote, then women, who were more capable of exercising the privilege, should have the same power.'*

# RATTRAY, LIZZIE FROST
## *1855–1931*

Lizzie Frost Fenton was born in Dunedin, New Zealand, on 22 March 1855, the daughter of Mary Lister and her husband, John Albert Fenton, an Anglican clergyman. She was educated in England and France, then returned to New Zealand to settle with her family in Oamaru.

In 1880 Lizzie Fenton moved to Auckland and took charge of the Young Women's Institute, a forerunner of the YWCA. In Auckland on 1 March 1883 she married William Rattray, a prominent Auckland draper. William was honorary secretary of the St John Ambulance Association and Lizzie shared her husband's involvement. She organised a street collection which raised the first funds of about £500 towards the purchase of the association's premises in Rutland Street.

A prominent member of St Luke's Anglican Church, Lizzie Rattray was an enthusiastic and able worker for a variety of welfare organisations. These included the St Barnabas' Association and Order of the Good Shepherd, and the Girls' Friendly Society which gave assistance to girls and young women immigrating to Auckland.

The winner of several prizes in short story competitions and an artist of 'considerable ability' who exhibited with the Auckland Society of Arts, Lizzie Rattray became one of New Zealand's earliest women journalists. For some years she was the New Zealand correspondent for the *Gentlewoman* magazine, and in 1892 Henry Brett invited her to assist with his *New Zealand Graphic*. Later, she became the journal's social editor and was able to use her position to influence the lives of women. Not only were there pages on fashion and social etiquette, but also discussions concerning controversial feminist issues such as the franchise and the involvement of women in a wider range of occupations and sporting activities. Although she was not associated with the temperance movement, Rattray condemned the effects on marriage of the 'terrible vice of intemperance'.

In 1892 Lizzie Rattray was elected to the committee of the Auckland branch of the Women's Franchise League. Her friend and close associate, Amey Daldy, was president. Rattray described members of the Auckland committee as 'mostly quiet, domesticated women, who would have preferred to still blush unseen at their own firesides, had not a burning sense of the injustice done to their sex by the one-sidedness of the present suffrage laws driven them to make an effort to obtain their rights'. She spoke publicly on women's employment, education and the justice of the franchise cause.

In June 1892 she proposed that men be allowed to sit on the league's committee and five were subsequently appointed. On 11 August 1893 Rattray and others presented to the House of Representatives a petition calling for the enfranchisement of women. In countering arguments against the entry of women into politics, she contended that 'Woman as she is may not be physically or morally capable of filling office ... but neither would it be expected that a man just released from long imprisonment would find the same facility in running a mile as the trained athlete.' She believed that younger women, whose minds had been allowed to develop, would be more fit to govern.

An influential Auckland citizen with a reputation as a compelling speaker, writer, administrator and social activist, Lizzie Rattray died in Parnell, Auckland, on 12 August 1931. She was survived by her husband and two sons.

*Theresa B. Graham*

Obit. *Auckland Star.* 12 Aug. 1931
Obit. *New Zealand Herald.* 14 Aug. 1931

# REYNOLDS, RACHEL SELINA
## *1838-1928*

Rachel Selina Pinkerton was born in South Australia on 19 December 1838, the eldest of six children of Eleanor Smith and her husband, William Pinkerton. Her childhood, delightfully described in her memoir, *Pioneering in Australia and New Zealand* (1929), was full of adventure. Her parents emigrated to Australia as newly-weds in 1838, establishing a sheep run near Adelaide. Just 36 hours after Rachel was born their new house and most of its contents – including a piano, 10 years' supply of clothing brought from England and the baby's delicately hand-sewn layette – were destroyed in a fire.

It was a lonely and violent place. Rachel's father was away for weeks at a time, and her mother sometimes had to barricade the door and hide her children under the table while she confronted 15 or 20 spear-carrying aboriginal warriors. When Rachel was about 10 years old the family moved to a less isolated location, Port Lincoln. She made new friends and developed new skills, such as wielding a stockwhip from horseback to drive wild cattle. For William Pinkerton, however, the move, far from providing greater security, was a disaster: 'his life was a torture – no security of life and limb', Rachel wrote. 'He had many cases of robbery, despoliation and murder as well.' The gruesome murder of one of his shepherds determined him to leave. He bought a 200-ton brig on which, in 1855, he took his family and as much stock as he could carry to Otago, New Zealand: 'a long and trying passage, out of both food and water for our sheep and selves', as Rachel tersely described it. It marked the end of a phase in her life, which would henceforward be much more sedate.

While William Pinkerton took his sheep to Tapanui and

OTAGO EARLY SETTLERS MUSEUM

*Speaking in support of women's franchise at a public meeting in Dunedin in 1891,
Rachel Reynolds asserted that 'very few people would in future say that woman had
no right to equality with man'. Rather, 'a great many would be sufficiently
noble to admit that woman had a right not only to be regarded as man's
equal but even as his superior.'*

set about clearing land and building a house, the family lived in Dunedin, walking long distances over unformed, muddy roads to join in the little town's social life. Since theirs was one of only two pianos in Dunedin it accompanied them to dances, on a horse-drawn sleigh.

On 7 October 1856, at Dunedin, 17-year-old Rachel Pinkerton married William Hunter Reynolds, a 34-year-old merchant. William Reynolds was by this time well established in business and launched on a career in local and national politics that would span 46 years. His background was as adventurous as that of his wife. He grew up in Portugal where he worked in his father's cork business; he bore scars from encounters with Spanish brigands. Shortly after the marriage Rachel accompanied her husband to England to recruit colonists. The stormy voyage was a nightmare for her, desperately seasick and pregnant; the first of her nine children (five daughters and four sons) was born in England.

Back in Dunedin the couple bought the fine hillside property of Montecillo, their home for nearly 40 years and the centre of Rachel Reynolds's life. She took pleasure in managing her large household. This busy, happy family period was disrupted when in 1868 her father's roving disposition caused him to leave his now flourishing West Otago estate for disastrous ventures in San Francisco and New Mexico.

While her family was still young Rachel Reynolds joined women's committees for the establishment of a girls' high school in Dunedin and for the admission of women to the University of Otago. Both of these objects were achieved in 1871. In 1879 she demonstrated her concern for disadvantaged children by taking part in an attempt to set up a crèche. Her charitable work stemmed from a religious faith nurtured by regular study of the Bible. She believed that 'no one can be living a truly Christian life who does not mingle frequently with the poor'. She distributed fresh fruit and vegetables daily from Montecillo, and every Sunday walked to the Otago Benevolent Institution to read to the old people there.

Much of her work focused on nearby St Andrew's Church,

which she and her husband helped found. Its dynamic minister, Rutherford Waddell, was a valued friend whose social conscience matched her own. Rachel Reynolds set up a Six-penny Clothing Club, to which subscribers donated 6d. a month and material to make clothing for poor families. She held weekly mothers' meetings where she taught young mothers to sew for themselves and their children; each of her daughters was given responsibility for one of the families. She enjoyed the company of the women, to whom she paid the courtesy of always dressing in her best. She took part in the agitation of 1889 against sweated labour conditions in Dune-din. When money was being raised for a women's ward at Dunedin Hospital she was on the committee.

It was to the free kindergarten movement that Rachel Reynolds devoted her chief energies. The impetus came from two sources: concern about the waifs of the notorious Walker Street (Carroll Street) area, which was near Montecillo, and the belief that early training 'with tenderness, sympathy and pity' could develop the 'all round possibilities lurking in every child'. As president of the Dunedin Free Kindergarten Assoc-iation she worked tirelessly with other enthusiasts to establish the Walker Street kindergarten, which opened with 14 child-ren in the Walker Street mission hall in June 1889. She lived to see the establishment of eight kindergartens, one of them bearing her name, with partial government funding.

Her commitment to social justice led Rachel Reynolds to support the extension of the franchise to women. At a crowded public meeting in 1891 she proposed a vote of thanks to its advocates in parliament. Woman, she said, had 'a right to equality with man in the very nature of things'. Notwithstand-ing her own strong religious affiliation she favoured the establishment of a women's franchise league unconnected with 'any church, sect, or temperance movement', and accept-ed the vice presidency of the league which was formed in Dunedin in April 1892. She affirmed that women needed the vote not 'merely because man had it, but in order to help the world to higher and nobler things.'

Rachel Reynolds fulfilled with ease and charm the social obligations imposed by her husband's position. In February 1896, for example, when the Intercolonial Medical Congress of Australasia, held in Dunedin, coincided with a vice-regal visit, she was hostess to an elaborate garden party for 500 guests. She was a woman of great intelligence as well as wide humanity, and despite having had only one year's formal schooling had the confidence to publish poems, lectures and even her views on the evolution debate, where she took the bold line: ''Tis Evolution holds the key / To that great fact, Divinity'.

After the death of William in 1899, Rachel Reynolds made three voyages to England. She handed over some of her charitable responsibilities, but maintained into old age her delight in helping others. She died at her daughter's home in Dunedin on 21 August 1928.

*Dorothy Page*

Harper, B. *Petticoat pioneers.* Book 3. Wellington, 1980

Obit. *Evening Star.* 22 Aug. 1928

[Turner, E. R.] 'Pioneer women'. *Woman To-day* (Aug. 1937): 26

MARY ASTLEY-FORD

*Annie Schnackenberg, speaking on the use of the vote at the 1894 Women's Christian Temperance Union convention, said 'let us ever be on the alert to take advantage of every opportunity for gaining information on matters of general interest, so that we may more intelligently exercise our privilege.'*

# SCHNACKENBERG, ANNIE JANE
## *1835–1905*

Annie Jane Allen was born probably on 22 November 1835 and baptised at Leamington Priors, Warwickshire, England, on 25 December 1835. She was the daughter of Elizabeth Dodd and Edward Allen, a businessman and farmer. Little is known of her early life. The Allens arrived in New Zealand on the *Black Eagle* in 1861 and settled at Mount Albert in Auckland.

Soon afterwards, the devoutly religious Annie Allen was asked by ex-missionary Eliza White to teach at the Wesleyan mission school at Kawhia on the west coast of the North Island. She agreed and went to the mission in November 1861. The arduous journey took a fortnight. She travelled by bullock dray to Mercer, by Maori canoe up the Waikato and Waipa rivers, on foot to the head of the Kawhia Harbour and then by canoe again to the mission station. At Kawhia she met Cort Henry Schnackenberg, a Wesleyan minister, whom she married in Auckland on 12 May 1864. Schnackenberg, a widower, had come to New Zealand in the 1830s via Australia from the German kingdom of Hanover. The couple were to have three daughters and two sons.

As well as dedicating herself to being a housewife, Annie Schnackenberg assisted her husband with mission duties. These included preaching at services, writing letters – particularly official communications with the government – and keeping the mission's accounts. Because the mission was expected to be self-sufficient, she grew fruit and vegetables and taught her female pupils how to sew their own clothes.

The Schnackenbergs had good relations with Maori; it is said that theirs was the first Pakeha house that King Tawhiao visited once fighting had ended in Waikato in 1864. Even so,

church authorities considered it too dangerous for the Schnackenbergs to continue living at the Kawhia mission on the edge
of the King Country because of a Kingite embargo on Pakeha
travelling into that region. They were transferred to Raglan.

On 10 August 1880 Cort Schnackenberg died and Annie
returned with their children to her parents' house in Auckland. She divided her time between church and Sunday school
work at the Pitt Street Wesleyan Church, and became involved
with Christian women's organisations.

Annie Schnackenberg was a founder member of the New
Zealand Women's Christian Temperance Union, established
in 1885. Because of her fluency in Maori, gained during her
time as a teacher at the mission schools in Kawhia and Raglan,
she was appointed superintendent of Maori work. The union
was disturbed at evidence of alcohol abuse among Maori and
placed great emphasis on proselytising Maori women.
Schnackenberg travelled to settlements such as Ohinemutu
and Whakarewarewa in the central North Island to advocate
temperance and the observation of the sabbath.

Annie Schnackenberg was national president of the
WCTU from 1892 to 1901 and became vice president-at-large
in 1901. She was president of the Auckland branch of the union
from 1887 to 1897. As one of the earliest advocates of temperance instruction in schools, she became superintendent of the
scientific temperance instruction department. During her
term in office temperance textbooks were ordered by the
Department of Education, making it possible, subject to the
approval of headmasters and local school committees, for
temperance to be taught in New Zealand schools.

The WCTU was at the forefront of the agitation for
women's suffrage in New Zealand, and it was during Schnackenberg's time as national president that women in this country
were granted the vote. Schnackenberg thought that this
achievement was just as important as the temperance aspect of
the WCTU's work. In 1893 she publicly thanked God for the
enfranchisement of women and suggested that members
should try to influence other women to make the best use of the

rights they had gained. In her opinion the vote was 'a sacred trust to be used for the advancement of every righteous cause.' However, her view of the future was not radical; she felt that universal suffrage alone was sufficient to ensure the equality of women and men and did not believe that women wanted to become members of Parliament.

Other WCTU reforms supported by Schnackenberg included the raising to 21 of the age of consent for girls and the repeal of the Contagious Diseases Act 1869, which made legal the compulsory examination of prostitutes (but not their clients) or women thought to be prostitutes. Any act of Parliament, she felt, which 'interferes with the rights and liberties of women only to make it safe for men to sin, is a disgrace to a community calling itself Christian'. Schnackenberg represented the WCTU at the inaugural meeting of the National Council of Women of New Zealand in Christchurch in 1896, where she was appointed a vice president. Her attendance at the annual sessions was not regular, but when present she spoke strongly in supporting the repeal of the Contagious Diseases Act.

Annie Schnackenberg was also a member of the YWCA, founded in Auckland in 1885. While on the board from 1890 to 1903, she worked on a social committee organising entertainment for the girls at the YWCA rooms and served as acting president (with Susie Mactier) from 1899 to 1901. Ill health prompted Annie Schnackenberg to give up the presidency of the WCTU in 1901. Serious illness in 1903 curtailed her involvement with the YWCA and she was an invalid for two years before her death in Auckland on 2 May 1905. She was remembered for her 'warm-hearted sincerity, unfailing good nature' and 'remarkable gift of common sense.'

*Megan Hutching*

Glasgow, K., ed. *A new earth.* Wellington, 1975
Obit. *White Ribbon* 11, No 121: 8

*Kate Sheppard warned the Women's Christian Temperance Union convention
in 1889 that 'while we have no hesitation in saying that all the truth and logic is on
our side, we must not forget that there is still a formidable barrier of prejudice to
break down, before the public mind will consent to women having
equal electoral privileges with men.'*

# SHEPPARD, KATHERINE WILSON
## *1847–1934*

Catherine Wilson Malcolm was born in Liverpool, Lancashire, England, probably on 10 March 1847, the daughter of Scots parents Jemima Crawford Souter and her husband, Andrew Wilson Malcolm, a clerk. She was called Catherine after her grandmother, but preferred to use the names Katherine or Kate. Her early childhood years were spent in London, Nairn in Scotland, and Dublin. A child of outstanding intellectual ability, she was well educated and her later writings reflect an extensive knowledge of the sciences, arts and the law. Her strong religious education and her adherence to religious principle and Christian socialism is attributed to the influence of an uncle, who was minister of the Free Church of Scotland in Nairn.

Her father died in 1862, and in 1868 her mother brought Katherine and her two brothers and a sister as saloon passengers to New Zealand; they arrived on the *Matoaka* at Lyttelton in February 1869. The family settled in Christchurch, where Katherine's sister, Marie Beath, was living. At Christchurch on 21 July 1871, Katherine, at the age of 24, married Walter Allen Sheppard, a grocer and general merchant. Their only son, Douglas, was born at Christchurch on 8 October 1880. During the early years of her marriage Katherine Sheppard was an active member of the Trinity Congregational Church, giving her time to church visiting, Bible classes and fund-raising. She became secretary of the Ladies Association, and was also involved with other members of her family in temperance work.

In 1885 Mary Leavitt, an evangelist delegate from the Woman's Christian Temperance Union of the United States of

America, commenced her mission in New Zealand and Kate Sheppard became a founding member of the New Zealand Women's Christian Temperance Union. It was quickly realised by the union that proposed social and legislative reforms concerning temperance and the welfare of women and children would be more effectively carried out if women possessed the right to vote and the right to representation in Parliament. In 1887 franchise departments were formed within the local unions and Sheppard was appointed national superintendent of the franchise and legislation department.

In this position she was responsible for co-ordinating and encouraging the local unions: she prepared and distributed pamphlets, wrote letters to the press and stimulated debate within the WCTU, church meetings, and temperance and political societies. An accomplished public speaker and writer, she had a clear, logical intellect, and could also conduct argument without rancour. Kate Sheppard was motivated by humanitarian principles and a strong sense of justice: 'All that separates, whether of race, class, creed, or sex, is inhuman, and must be overcome'. Hers was a quietly determined, persuasive and disarmingly feminine voice.

Kate was accompanied on her speaking engagements by her younger sister, Isabella May, who worked with her as superintendent of the literature department of the WCTU. The pamphlets distributed by the union were sent to members of Parliament. The temperance societies, already strongly organised within the community, believed that if women had the vote there would be a national majority in favour of prohibition. The emphasis throughout the campaign, however, was on the right of women to vote; that right had previously been extended to males over 21 years. Women, in being excluded, had been classed with juveniles, lunatics and criminals.

The franchise department of the WCTU took the first of three major petitions to Parliament in 1891. The petition was presented by Sir John Hall, and strongly supported by Alfred Saunders and the premier, John Ballance. It was signed by more than 9,000 women, and the second in 1892 by more than 19,000.

In June 1891 Kate Sheppard inaugurated and began editing a women's page in the *Prohibitionist*, the national temperance magazine. With the formation of franchise leagues in many centres, and the increasing activity and growth of the WCTU auxiliaries in the smaller centres, the largest petition ever presented to Parliament was collected in 1893 with nearly 32,000 signatures. The small band of 600 women members of the WCTU had successfully roused public opinion to the extent that Parliament could no longer ignore their demands.

The Electoral Act 1893 was passed on 19 September and Kate Sheppard received a telegram from the premier, Richard Seddon, previously her political enemy in the House, conceding victory to the women. The governor, Lord Glasgow, honoured Kate Sheppard as a political leader, by symbolically presenting to her the pen with which the bill granting womanhood suffrage had been signed.

It was ten weeks before the election, and the WCTU set about enrolling women. Kate Sheppard emphasised that the franchise department of the WCTU was anxious for all women of all classes to enrol. Sixty-five per cent of all New Zealand women over 21 voted in the first election. New Zealand had become the first country in which all women exercised the right to vote.

In 1894 Kate Sheppard returned with her husband and son to England where she met other leading feminists and with tireless energy joined in a hectic round of public speaking and debate in support of women's franchise. New life had been infused into the women's suffrage movement in England by the success and encouragement of the New Zealand campaigners. Sheppard attended the World's Woman's Christian Temperance Union biennial convention in London in June 1895 as New Zealand's delegate and met that union's president, Frances Willard. Her speeches were reported in British as well as New Zealand newspapers.

While in London Kate Sheppard was requested by the

International Council of Women to form a national council of women in New Zealand. On her return to Christchurch she found that the Canterbury Women's Institute had already called a meeting of the franchise leagues and other women's societies, in order to form a federation of women's organisations. It was decided to make this April 1896 meeting the inaugural session of the National Council of Women of New Zealand, and Kate Sheppard was elected president, a position she held for the next three years.

Sheppard's absence had resulted in some disarray among her supporters in the House. A bill to include women's representation in Parliament was thwarted by her two previous stalwarts, Alfred Saunders and Sir John Hall, who wanted a separate chamber for women. Kate Sheppard had never advocated a separationist policy, and the loss of her influence meant, perhaps, that the crucial moment for women's complete political equality was also lost.

The annual conferences of the NCW, often called the 'Women's Parliament', were frequently reported with full coverage by the local daily papers, and the resolutions passed were covered by the national press. These meetings also became an arena for public debate on social issues and affairs of state. In her presidential address at the second session in Christchurch in 1897 Kate Sheppard stated: 'In Wellington is every year assembled a National Council of men, which holds a session lasting several months. ... From that Council women are excluded. ... Under these circumstances a National Council which largely represents the thinking and working women of the colony (and which, it may be remarked, costs the country nothing) becomes a necessity. I trust the day is not far distant ... when the necessity for men's councils and women's councils, as such, will be swept away.'

In 1895 the WCTU began publishing its own newspaper, the *White Ribbon*, which was then the only paper in New Zealand to be started, owned, edited, managed and published by women. Under the editorship of Kate Sheppard this became the 'Hansard' of both the WCTU and the NCW. Its 16 pages were used to keep the branch unions informed of activities, to co-ordinate and report on organisations affiliated with the NCW and to conduct the ongoing campaign for the creation of a just society within the ideals of Christian socialism. Articles were included on health and rational dress, education, education against alcohol, women's political and legal disabilities, and equal wages for women.

Many of these articles were written by Sheppard. Often published as separate pamphlets, they reveal the coherence of her social philosophy. In lucid prose she discusses the need to make full use of women's suffrage in New Zealand, repeal the Contagious Diseases Act 1869, emphasise the responsibilities of women as citizens, promote economic independence for married women, reform government and reconsider the guardianship of children. It is clear that she regarded the family as the foundation of the state, and believed that the state should therefore serve families. With regard to the position of women in the family, she asked: 'If the mother is dwarfed, repressed, how can the children grow to their full mental and moral stature?' In her view there was 'no greater anomaly than the exaltation by men of the vocation of wife and mother on the one hand, while, on the other, the position is by law stripped of all its attractiveness and dignity, and a wife and mother is regarded not only as a "dependent" on her husband's bounty, but even the children of her own body are regarded as his legal property.' The practical means of ending a wife's economic and legal dependence on her husband was given in the NCW proposal that there should be a law 'attaching a certain just share of the husband's earnings or income' for the wife's separate use, 'payable if she so desires it, into her own account.'

Kate Sheppard translated her political philosophy into practical proposals for reform. These largely followed the Swiss model, and were supported by Alfred Saunders. They included proportional representation, with non-party affiliation; the initiative and referendum, whereby the public would have the right to initiate or veto legislation; and the elective executive, whereby cabinet ministers would be elected by all members of Parliament. The cabinet was to be a consultative body whose members would be persons of moral character, ability and experience who would be concerned to co-operate for the common good. To prevent any individual from dominating excessively, the prime minister was viewed as a chairperson, voted in for a one-year term.

Kate Sheppard's most active years as a political leader for social reform were from 1887 to 1902. During this period she was franchise and legislation superintendent of the WCTU, convener of the economics department of the Canterbury Women's Institute, and from 1896 to 1902 president or vice president of the NCW. After eight strenuous years as editor and contributor to the *White Ribbon* she resigned at the Dunedin WCTU convention in April 1903, owing to ill health and the pending retirement of her husband, Walter Sheppard, who wished to settle in England. Before she departed in July 1903 to join Walter and son Douglas, who was attending the University of London, she was publicly honoured by the executive of the NCW for her outstanding contribution to the community.

She travelled to England through Canada and the United States where she met Carrie Chapman Catt and other leading feminists. With an improvement in her health she was able to attend some public functions in London where she was in demand as a public speaker. Although she wrote a number of letters to the editors of national newspapers on the debate on women's suffrage, her health again steadily declined and she was unable to attend the International Council of Women's quinquennial meeting in Berlin in 1904. Her paper, however, was read to the 19 national councils represented at the meeting.

After an unsuccessful attempt at a rest cure, Kate Sheppard was advised by her doctors that she would need to spend the winters in the south of France. She chose instead to return to New Zealand and arrived back with her husband in September 1904. In March 1905 Margaret Sievwright, then president of the NCW, died. Although an attempt was made to continue the council's work by electing new officers with Kate Sheppard as president, the council went into recess in 1906. That same year Sheppard declined the office of franchise superintendent of the World's WCTU. She lived quietly, retiring from public speaking, but continued to influence the women's movement through her writing and work with the franchise and legislation department of the New Zealand WCTU, and by acting in an advisory capacity to the *White Ribbon*. In 1909, at the Toronto quinquennial meeting of the International Council of Women, Kate Sheppard was elected honorary vice president, even though she was unable to attend.

On 29 June 1908 in Edinburgh, Scotland, Kate Sheppard's son, Douglas, married Wilhelmina Sievwright, daughter of her friend and co-worker, Margaret Sievwright. Douglas Sheppard died soon afterwards, on 16 March 1910. Walter Sheppard died in Bath, England, on 24 July 1915.

In 1916 Kate Sheppard, Christina Henderson and Jessie Mackay met with the intention of reconvening the National Council of Women. Personal letters were sent to women in the various centres; local branch councils were formed in the main centres. Kate Sheppard was unable to attend the first conference of the revived council in Wellington in 1919, but her address, written in her capacity as founding president, was read for her. She was made a national life member in 1923.

At Christchurch on 15 August 1925, aged 78, Kate Sheppard married William Sidney Lovell-Smith, a 72-year-old printer and author of *Outlines of the women's franchise movement in New Zealand*; he died four years later. Her only grandchild, Margaret Isobel Sheppard, died in 1930. Kate Lovell-Smith died at her home at Riccarton, Christchurch, on 13 July 1934, and was buried in Addington cemetery with her mother, a brother and a sister. The *Christchurch Times* reported her death in simple appreciation: 'A great woman has gone, whose name will remain an inspiration to the daughters of New Zealand while our history endures.'

*Tessa K. Malcolm*

Grimshaw, P. *Women's suffrage in New Zealand.* Auckland, 1972

Mackay, J. 'Pioneer women: a portrait of Kate Wilson Sheppard, first president of the National Council of Women'. *Woman To-day* (April 1937): 2–3

Obit. *Christchurch Times.* 16 July 1934

Sheppard, C. W. Papers, 1870–1916. MS. CMU

# SIEVWRIGHT, MARGARET HOME
## *1844-1905*

Margaret Richardson, later known as Margaret Home Richardson, was born at Pencaitland, East Lothian, Scotland, on 19 March 1844, the daughter of Jane Law Home and her husband, John Richardson, an estate factor. In her youth she taught deprived children in the ragged schools of Edinburgh. She then trained as a nurse, working in hospitals under the Florence Nightingale system, and joined Josephine Butler's campaign for the repeal of the contagious diseases acts of 1864, 1866 and 1869.

In the 1870s Margaret Richardson emigrated to New Zealand, and on 29 November 1878 at Wellington she married William Sievwright, a solicitor from Lerwick, Shetland islands, who worked at the legal firm of Sievwright and Stout. William already had two daughters by his first marriage and the couple were to have one more. Margaret's father also joined their household. In 1883 the Sievwrights moved to Gisborne where William established his own practice. They bought a property on the hills overlooking the town and Poverty Bay in 1884. That year the Married Women's Property Act was passed and it is significant that the land title was registered in Margaret's name.

Margaret Sievwright was a tall, fine-looking woman with a retiring, sensitive nature that made her averse to involvement in public affairs. Her frail appearance belied the energy and tenacity with which she fought injustice and defended the rights of women and children. She was intelligent, well educated and articulate, and was encouraged by a liberal, supportive husband. After she had set up a small school on their property, she joined a benevolent society, which organised

GISBORNE MUSEUM

*'We have reached one milestone, it is true, the milestone of the suffrage; we pause, but only again to press forward.' Margaret Sievwright in an address to the Gisborne Woman's Political Association in 1894.*

funds for community projects such as isolation wards for the local hospital, and a home for aged men.

Margaret Sievwright was appointed to the Waiapu Licensing Board and she organised the Gisborne branch of the New Zealand Women's Christian Temperance Union, the national organisation that was deeply involved with the suffrage movement in New Zealand. Along with other national leaders, Sievwright maintained strong connections with feminist movements overseas.

Between 1887 and 1892, despite continuous agitation, several women's franchise bills failed. In 1893 suffragists, headed by Kate Sheppard and Margaret Sievwright, took a petition of nearly 32,000 signatures to their leading pro-suffrage supporter, Sir John Hall. He presented the petition to the House of Representatives, and despite the obstruction of Premier Richard Seddon, the Electoral Bill finally became law. Women's political organisations undertook the task of educating women to use the vote effectively and influence legislation. In 1894 Sievwright convened the Gisborne Women's Political Association which she represented at the National Council of Women of New Zealand, formed by former suffragists in 1896 to co-ordinate the various women's groups. She was a vice president up to 1901, when she became president until her death in 1905. She established and was secretary of the Local Council of Waiapu Women in 1901 and was president from 1902 to 1904. The aims of this society were, first, to promote the further enfranchisement of women, and second, to bring individual women into touch with national and international women's movements. Sievwright's feminist vision was perhaps best expressed in a speech of 1900: 'The question is often asked, "What do women want?" We want men "to stand out of our sunshine"; that is all.'

Margaret Sievwright believed that broader emancipation could only be achieved through supporting political parties that promised to further the interests of women. She was an idealist aiming at total equality for all women. She wanted economic independence for married women, equal pay, and sex instruction and education for parenthood. She fought for the reform of the marriage and divorce laws, and maintained that prostitution would always exist as long as women lacked equal opportunity in employment. She objected to the stigma of the word 'illegitimate'. Sievwright worked for disarmament during the South African war (1899–1902), and condemned any project 'likely to involve Australasia in the participation of warfare'. For these beliefs she was castigated by the press.

By 1903 she realised the fire had gone out of the women's movement and complained that 'the apathy and cheerful indifference of the great majority is distinctly benumbing'. She prophesied rightly that it would take a long, hard struggle to rekindle it.

Margaret Sievwright died at Whataupoko, Poverty Bay, on 9 March 1905. Her husband, William, died in 1909. Their daughter Wilhelmina married Kate Sheppard's only child, Douglas Sheppard, in 1908. Margaret Sievwright's fellow workers recognised her life of self-sacrifice and devotion to the cause of women's advancement by erecting a monument to her in Peel Street, Gisborne, in 1906. An inscription reads, 'Ever a friend to the friendless, an uncompromising upholder of all that is merciful, temperate and just.'

*Elspeth M. Simpson*

Gregory, F. 'Margaret Home Sievwright, radical, practical, visionary'. *Gisborne Herald*. 14 Sept. 1984

Grimshaw, P. *Women's suffrage in New Zealand*. Auckland, 1972

Holt, B. *et al. Women in council*. Wellington, 1980

# SMITH, LUCY MASEY
## *1861–1936*

Lucy Masey Smith was born in Christchurch, New Zealand, on 1 June 1861. She was the fifth of six children of Eleanor Phoebe Macleod and her husband, James Thomas Smith, a compositor. The family had emigrated from England the previous year. Lucy attended St Albans Wesleyan day school where she won prizes for spelling and reading. Her parents were staunch members of the St Albans Wesleyan Church, and church activities played a major part in their family life. Lucy joined the church's Sunday school, Bible class and choir, often performing as an alto soloist with the choir in the 1880s.

Lucy Smith began teacher training at the Christchurch Normal School, but withdrew in the latter part of 1879 due to ill health. By this time her father had established a printing business and built a printing factory next to the family home in Springfield Road. He began publishing the magazine *New Zealand Titbits* in 1885; Lucy's mother was the editor.

Eleanor Phoebe Smith was a feminist who joined the New Zealand Women's Christian Temperance Union (WCTU) and the Canterbury Women's Institute. Lucy Smith also belonged to these organisations and she supported the campaigns for women's rights and suffrage. Her interest in women's issues and her likely experience in the printing and publishing business were happily combined in 1894 when she became editor of the WCTU's page in the *Prohibitionist*, writing under the pen-name 'Vesta'. The page had hitherto been edited by the suffrage leader Kate Sheppard, who was paying a visit to England.

The following year Lucy Smith and other WCTU members established the *White Ribbon*, a monthly magazine. It

*'We do not for a moment imagine that women alone are capable of framing laws
which shall be perfectly fair and just to men as well as to women;
why then should we demand so much more of men?' Editorial comment by
Lucy Smith in the Women's Christian Temperance Union page of
the* Prohibitionist, *11 August 1894.*

CANTERBURY MUSEUM

was published by the WCTU, and printed by Smith, Anthony, Sellars and Company, the family printing business now managed by Lucy's brother William Sidney Smith. Lucy Smith was appointed associate editor of the *White Ribbon* and Kate Sheppard, who returned to New Zealand in 1896, was appointed editor.

Smith attended the first meeting of the National Council of Women of New Zealand (NCW) in 1896. Unlike most of the other women activists, she was in paid employment: on her father's death in 1896 she took up office duties and remained working at the family printing business as proofreader until about 1920.

In 1903 Kate Sheppard resigned as editor of the *White Ribbon*, Mary Jane (Jennie) Smith, the wife of William Sidney Smith, resigned as business manager, and Lucy Smith took over both positions. For five years she produced the magazine, maintaining a similar editorial policy to that adopted by Kate Sheppard. Her associate editor during this period was the writer Jessie Mackay.

At the same time, she continued to serve as a Sunday school teacher and young ladies' Bible class leader at St Albans Wesleyan Church. She attended leaders' meetings and became a congregational steward. After her mother's death in 1913, Lucy and her sister Eleanor continued to live in the family home on Papanui Road. In 1917, after the NCW was revived, Lucy Smith became an associate member of the Christchurch branch, and in 1927 became its secretary. From 1928 to 1929 she edited the NCW's *Bulletin* magazine.

A combination of poor health, a heavy workload and a retiring disposition meant that Lucy Smith was not a leader in the women's movement; her work was always done quietly, behind the scenes. In 1902 the *White Ribbon* had commented that 'Much of her work, even on this paper, has been unappreciated because it has been unknown'. Yet a study of her writing shows that she was a strong feminist, progressive thinker, and courageous reformer who cared deeply about social issues and was prepared to espouse unpopular viewpoints.

Lucy Smith followed her brother's family in changing her name to Lovell-Smith in 1926. She never married. She died at her home in St Albans on 3 March 1936.

*Margaret Lovell-Smith*

Lovell-Smith family papers. MS. CMU

National Council of Women of New Zealand. Christchurch Branch. Records, 1896–1970. MS. CU

Obit. *Press.* 4 March 1936

# STOUT, ANNA PATERSON
## *1858–1931*

Anna Paterson Logan was born at Ferntree Cottage, Royal Terrace, Dunedin, New Zealand, on 29 September 1858, the daughter of Jessie Alexander Pollock and her husband, John Logan. Her Scottish parents had settled in Dunedin in 1854, and at the time of Anna's birth John Logan was clerk to the superintendent of the Otago province.

Anna Logan was brought up in a comfortable yet questioning family, with a keen sense of social and personal duty. John and Jessie Logan belonged to the temperance and freethought movements; they believed in the development of individual human potential and the perfectibility of society. When she was 12 Anna sat and passed the entrance examination to the Girls' Provincial School. The high standards of womanly propriety and service set by the first headmistress, Margaret Burn, gave Anna ideals by which she measured her own and others' behaviour for the rest of her life. These ideals, Anna claimed in 1921, were 'devoid of all snobbery, and were founded upon a clear estimate of the value of character and strength of purpose necessary to the attainment of true womanhood.'

After leaving school Anna lived at home until, in Dunedin on 27 December 1876, aged 18, she married Robert Stout, a 32-year-old barrister and member of the House of Representatives. Robert, a fellow Scot, had been a frequent visitor and had discussed freethought and the problems of the world with the Logans; he had strong opinions and was a supporter of women's rights. Anna accompanied Robert to Wellington for the 1877 Parliamentary session. He became attorney general in March 1878.

'The real power of the woman's vote in New Zealand is not in opposition, but in its harmony and co-operation with the men's vote.' From Woman suffrage in New Zealand by Anna Stout (London, 1911).

Neither Robert's political career nor his legal practice progressed smoothly. Anna had to get used to moves between Dunedin and Wellington and a family life punctuated by financial and professional crises. Between 1878 and 1894 she gave birth to six children whom she cared for with the assistance of domestic staff. She supported her husband in his political career – a particularly demanding task when he was premier from 1884 to 1887 – and developed her own political and social views.

Anna Stout's beliefs were strongly influenced by her husband and by his mentor and friend, Duncan MacGregor. The two men followed a liberal creed of individualism, progress through education, sexual equality and independence. Prohibition and social purity were also important goals in the social policy that Robert and Anna shared.

Anna Stout's philosophy was that women should have equal rights with men and be free to develop their intellectual ability to its highest capacity. Women had a right to take part in the life and work of the colony, but she initially believed that most women would exercise this right through their influence on husbands and children. Family and domestic responsibilities, which Anna put first, limited what she could do for herself and for the women's movement.

Although she had joined the New Zealand Women's Christian Temperance Union in 1885, it was not until the 1890s that she began to play a tentative, independent public role. In April 1892 she was elected president of the Women's Franchise League in Dunedin; the active leadership was provided by Marion Hatton. Early in 1895 Eva McLaren, corresponding secretary of the International Council of Women, approached Stout to preside over a New Zealand branch. She hesitated because of her family duties, her poor hearing and indifferent health. Although she finally agreed to accept the presidency if Kate Sheppard became secretary and did the work, Anna Stout was not elected to the position when the National Council of Women of New Zealand was established at a Christchurch convention in 1896. Instead she

became a vice president with Kate Sheppard as president. The
following year she had a public dispute with the council over
the venue of the annual convention and did not attend,
although scheduled to present a paper on the responsibilities of
parents. With this defection Stout weakened her links to the
main body of politically active women. The estrangement was
a pity because she had much in common with the women of the
National Council, and if she had remained with the organisation both it and she may have benefited.

Anna Stout attended the 1896 convention of women as the
representative of the Southern Cross Society, a Wellington
organisation she had helped found. The society aimed at
educating women politically, promoting their independence
and equality, and improving the living conditions of women
who worked for wages. Stout's agenda in such organisations
was to achieve gradual social and political change. Her view
was that women must learn to understand political institutions
and political economy before they could criticise governments.
Men and women, she believed, should receive equal pay for
equal work, but if women could not compete in an occupation
with men they must be prepared to leave it. Women should sit
in Parliament, but only when they were equally qualified with
men, and women should vote for politicians whose private and
public characters were without stain.

As part of the advancement of women, and hence of
society, Anna Stout supported the social purity movement,
popular among women reformers in England and America as
well as New Zealand. The movement aimed at the acceptance
of a single code of sexual behaviour – 'a white life for two' –
which, it was thought, would combat the problems of physical
degeneration (commonly attributed to sexually transmitted
diseases) and unhappy marriages. Stout also helped to found
the Wellington branch of the New Zealand Society for the
Protection of Women and Children in 1897.

In 1899 Robert Stout became chief justice and Anna
Stout's voice was once again silenced. It would have been a
breach of propriety for her to have taken a lead in social or

political matters. Her next chance for independence came in 1909 when she and Robert took their children to England. When Robert returned to New Zealand in 1910, Anna remained in England, where her children were studying, for a further two years. The British suffrage movement was going through a period of intense activity on the streets and in Parliament. As a representative of women voters, she was an object of curiosity and of use to the British campaigners.

Freed from the constraints of her New Zealand role, while still enjoying its status, Anna Stout aligned herself with the Women's Social and Political Union (WSPU), the militant wing of British suffragism founded by Emmeline and Christabel Pankhurst in 1903. In October 1909 Adela Pankhurst, in the WSPU newspaper *Votes for Women*, described Stout as a 'charming lady' with 'a boundless enthusiasm and a beautiful devotion to the cause of womanhood'. Stout had reassured her interviewer that the vote had not led New Zealand women to neglect their domestic duties, that women were as patriotic as men, that they had voted safely and that their votes had led to legislation improving the position of women and children. Replying to *The Times*'s anti-suffrage correspondents became one of Anna Stout's responsibilities. Her most notable encounter was with Lord Glasgow, who as governor of New Zealand had signed the legislation giving women the vote. Glasgow's claim that women's suffrage was a disaster, she asserted, insulted all the women of New Zealand.

Anna Stout's articles appeared in *Votes for Women* and the *Englishwoman* and were republished as leaflets and pamphlets by several suffrage associations. Because New Zealand was a world leader in women's suffrage, its example was looked to by both supporters and opponents of the vote. Stout felt ardently that if the world were to be reformed, it would be through the political power of women. She argued that in New Zealand the women's vote had never been a 'sex vote', but was won and exercised in harmony and co-operation with the men's vote. She refuted claims that women had not wanted the vote and did not use it, and that the women's vote had led to a decline in the birth rate and to economic ruin. Suffragists of all persuasions found her an appealing advocate.

London was a personal liberation for Stout. Not only did she engage in public controversy, but she marched through the streets behind WSPU banners and appeared on platforms in huge demonstrations in Hyde Park. Her papers, bequeathed to the Hocken Library, show the importance to her of this phase of her life.

Returning to Wellington, aged 54, Anna Stout settled into the role of a prominent club woman, taking part in the English-Speaking Union, the Wellington Pioneer Club, the Wellington Lyceum Club, the Wellington Women's Club, and, during the war, the Women's National Reserve of New Zealand. In 1917 she was involved in the revival of the National Council of Women and after the war became a member of the League of Nations Union of New Zealand. She occasionally engaged in public debates over the role of women. In 1917 she opposed proposals to emphasise domestic training in the education of girls.

More controversially, in 1918, she led a protest campaign against a police raid on a Wellington house and the subsequent trial of five women for allegedly running a brothel. Her main concern was that putting the women on trial while the men involved went free perpetuated the old double standard. In 1922, at the height of a wave of concern over the incidence of venereal disease, Anna Stout, fearing the reintroduction of compulsory medical examination of women suspected of prostitution, published a pamphlet opposing medical authorities who were demanding compulsory notification of the disease. Both campaigns showed Stout consistently following her belief in sexual equality.

Through the 1920s Anna Stout suffered from poor health and became less and less active. Her husband died on 19 July 1930 and she survived him by less than a year. She died on 10 May 1931 at Hanmer Springs, aged 72. She had led a life at the cutting edge of change in women's public role. As a woman of social standing and political influence, she was strategically placed to negotiate for women's advancement and this she had done, publicly when she could, and at other times privately.

*Raewyn Dalziel*

Dunn, W. H. & I. L. M. Richardson. *Sir Robert Stout.* Wellington, 1961

Stout, A. P. Books, newspaper clippings and papers, 1831–1930. MSS 244–278. DUHO

"For God, and Home, and Humanity."

# MINUTES

OF THE

## New Zealand

# WOMEN'S CHRISTIAN TEMPERANCE UNION,

AT THE

## FIRST ANNUAL MEETING,

## HELD IN WELLINGTON,

### 23rd FEBRUARY, 1886.

CONTAINING THE

### GENERAL AND LOCAL FORMS OF CONSTITUTION,

### BALANCE-SHEET,

AND

### REPORTS OF THE LOCAL UNIONS.

PRICE: FOURPENCE.

WELLINGTON:
LYON & BLAIR, PRINTERS, LAMBTON QUAY.
1886.

*Anne Ward presided over the first annual convention of the New Zealand Women's Christian Temperance Union in 1886; the minutes of that meeting recorded a resolution that the union should work for women's franchise.*

# WARD, ANNE
## *1825/26?–1896*

Anne Titboald was born, probably in 1825 or 1826, at Exeter, Devonshire, England, the daughter of Thomas Titboald; her mother's name is not known. She arrived on the *Cordelia* at Wellington, New Zealand, on 29 September 1854 with her lawyer husband, Charles Dudley Robert Ward (known as Dudley). They had married in Rotherhithe, Surrey, on 26 January 1850. The couple appear to have had no children.

Little is known of Anne Ward's early years in New Zealand. The couple probably lived in Wellington from the time of their arrival until 1868. Dudley Ward was elected MHR for Wellington Country district in 1855, and appointed chairman of the Courts of Sessions of the Peace for part of the province of Wellington in 1857. In September 1868 he was appointed temporary judge of the Supreme Court in Dunedin and it is likely that Anne Ward accompanied her husband there. In 1886 Dudley Ward was appointed to the same position in Auckland, a position he also held in Christchurch in 1887 and Dunedin again in 1894.

Anne Ward, or Mrs Dudley Ward as she was more commonly referred to, was the first national president of the New Zealand Women's Christian Temperance Union. The WCTU was established in New Zealand in 1885 by Mary Leavitt, an organiser from the Woman's Christian Temperance Union of the United States of America, who encouraged Ward to take a leadership role. Between September 1885 and January 1886 Ward travelled through the country delivering lectures on temperance and the work of the WCTU and established branches of the union in Wellington, Nelson, New Plymouth, Patea, Hawera, Wanganui and Ashburton.

The fundamental aim of the WCTU was to achieve prohibition of the sale and consumption of alcohol. As a means to this end, the union supported the goal of women's suffrage. It was felt that if women were involved in political decision-making, liquor laws were more likely to be changed. At the first annual convention of the WCTU in Wellington in February 1886, over which Anne Ward presided, a paper on votes for women was presented and delegates resolved that 'the union endeavour to obtain women's suffrage'. A franchise and legal department was established to promote this reform. At the same convention Ward was elected president and became superintendent of the evangelistic department, as well as being made organising agent for the union. At a public meeting during the convention she made a 'powerful appeal to any of her hearers who might happen to be moderate drinkers, to give up the habit.' She also gave details of the work that the union was doing in New Zealand, which included visiting gaols and poor people, conducting Bible classes, and work among 'fallen women'.

Anne Ward's motivation for becoming a member of the temperance movement was religious. When she first became involved with the WCTU in Wellington someone reminded her of her public position as a judge's wife, to which she replied that her position was that of a servant of Christ. On another occasion, at a meeting in Wellington in 1886, she spoke on the influence of alcohol on crime, asserting that it was 'useless to combat the drink evil without the assistance of Christ.'

The WCTU was keen to establish temperance kindergartens for children, aged from two to five years, of working mothers. At the annual convention in Christchurch in 1887 Ward spoke of the need for such a kindergarten in Auckland. She proposed engaging a teacher, who was to be paid £100 a year from money raised by 10s. subscriptions paid by members of the public. The Jubilee Kindergarten and Crèche was founded in Auckland in 1887, very much as a result of Ward's determination. By the following year an average of 90 children a day were being fed a hot meal, six days a week. It was handsomely supported by James Dilworth, who made an annual donation of £100. By the end of its first year of operation the kindergarten, which was run by a committee of women, employed four teachers as well as a matron.

In 1887 Anne Ward resigned as national president of the WCTU; her health had not been good for many years. She died on 31 May 1896 aged 70, at her home in Christchurch. Dudley Ward died on 30 August 1913. One obituary praised her for 'the interest she took in the welfare of the poor and in religious matters.' But possibly her most notable achievement was to establish, almost single-handedly, a national organisation which would spearhead significant social and political reforms.

*Megan Hutching*

Grimshaw, P. *Women's suffrage in New Zealand.* Auckland, 1972

New Zealand Women's Christian Temperance Union. *Minutes of the New Zealand Women's Christian Temperance Union at the first annual meeting.* Wellington, 1886

Obit. *Lyttelton Times.* 2 June 1896

*At the National Council of Women conference in 1898, Ada Wells advocated
economic as well as political independence for women on the grounds that
'a wife is an individual equally with her husband, and as such she
is entitled to the rights of an individual.'*

# WELLS, ADA
## *1863–1933*

Ada Pike was born at Shepherd's Green, near Henley-on-Thames, Oxfordshire, England, on 29 April 1863, the daughter of Maria Beckett and her husband, William Henry Pike, a journeyman wheelwright. In 1873 she travelled on the *Merope* with her parents, three sisters and one brother to New Zealand. The family arrived at Lyttelton on 31 October.

Ada attended Avonside School (which became part of Christchurch East School) from 1874, where, under the tuition of Henry Hill, she quickly showed her natural talents for Classics and languages. In 1876 she attended Christchurch West School and from 1877 to 1881 was employed there as a pupil-teacher. In 1881 she was awarded the university junior scholarship; she attended Canterbury College and passed the first part of her BA in 1882. For a short period she was employed as an assistant teacher under Helen Connon at Christchurch Girls' High School. Here she strove to pass on to her pupils her love of music, poetry and languages.

On 7 January 1884 she married Harry Wells, an organist, at Christchurch; they were to have three daughters and one son. Harry's volatile temper and continual drinking meant that he was unable to hold steady employment, and Ada was often forced to take sole responsibility for the economic and emotional support of her family. She took teaching positions and accepted private patients for massage and healing. It was said that her delicate, sensitive hands 'possessed a healing touch that came from the depths of her spirit.'

By the late 1880s an active campaign for women's enfranchisement was being organised. Ada Wells had always held strong beliefs on women's rights and the suffrage campaign enabled her to put her theories into action. While Kate Sheppard provided a public face to the cause, Wells's talents as a fervent, efficient organiser and campaigner were invaluable to the women's suffrage movement – talents recognised both by Sheppard and the movement as a whole.

When women won the vote Wells realised that this victory was merely the first in a long battle to achieve equality for women. While many of the suffrage campaigners retired from public life after 1893, Wells continued to take an active role in local and national politics. She argued in favour of free kindergartens, universal access to secondary education, the repeal of the Contagious Diseases Act 1869, and the reform of local government, the charitable aid system and prisons.

In 1892 Ada Wells, with Professor Alexander Bickerton, founded the Canterbury Women's Institute, of which she was president for many years. This was one of many offices she was to hold. In 1896 she became the first national secretary of the National Council of Women of New Zealand, and in 1898 she helped to spearhead the campaign for the formation of the Canterbury Children's Aid Society. In 1899 she became one of the first two women to be elected to the Ashburton and North Canterbury United Charitable Aid Board, serving as a member until 1906 in spite of the antagonism of male members of the board to her presence. In addition to this she was associated with the Prison-gate Mission, an organisation engaged in the rehabilitation of prisoners. She was a member of the National Peace Council of New Zealand and worked with groups providing aid to conscientious objectors during the First World War.

Ada Wells was also active in the campaign to amend the electoral law to enable women to be elected to Parliament. In 1917 she stood as a Labour candidate and became the first woman to be elected to the Christchurch City Council; this is perhaps how she is best remembered.

Ada Wells died at Christchurch on 22 March 1933, survived by her four children. Harry had died in 1918. In her lifetime she was to become a prominent and, at times, controversial public figure. She played a pivotal role in the advancement of women and was a tireless campaigner in the fight for women's equality and economic independence. Her views were no doubt strengthened by her marital experience. Wells's contribution to Christchurch, especially in the interests of women and children, was invaluable and sadly is often overlooked.

*Philippa Fogarty*

Grimshaw, P. A. 'Wells, Ada'. In *An encyclopaedia of New Zealand.* Ed. A. H. McLintock. Wellington, 1966

Obit. *Press.* 23 March 1933

'Pioneer women: the first secretary of the National Council'. *Woman To-day* (June 1937): 50

*'With regard to all powers, rights, and duties of citizens, absolute equality should be the law of the land.' Jessie Williamson moving that women should be able to sit in Parliament and take public office, at the National Council of Women conference in 1898.*

# WILLIAMSON, JESSIE MARGUERITE

*1855-57?–1937*

Jessie Marguerite McAllan was born in Dublin, Ireland, probably sometime between 1855 and 1857. She was the daughter of John McAllan, a merchant; her mother's identity is unknown. No information survives about Jessie's early life. On 11 December 1875 she married Hugh Bellis Williamson, a mercantile clerk, in Dublin. Around two years later the couple settled in Wanganui, New Zealand, and the first of their four daughters, Lena, was born. From about 1879 Hugh Williamson ran a chemist shop in Victoria Avenue.

Jessie Williamson was a principal member of the Wanganui Women's Franchise League (later renamed the Wanganui Women's Political League), which was established in May 1893 to co-ordinate locally the campaign for women's suffrage. She was treasurer in 1896, and either president or secretary from 1897 until 1903. In 1895 she and two other league members formed a deputation to the premier, Richard Seddon, to discuss the need for equal participation by both sexes in the civil service and equal pay for women and men.

Williamson was also active nationally, and as the league's delegate was a founding member in 1896 of the National Council of Women of New Zealand (NCW). In her report back to the league she declared that it was an unqualified mistake to admit participation of men at the first meeting of the council 'as it proved an opportunity for those with an "axe to grind" . . . to air their views . . . all the humbug that had been talked had been by men.' At the 1897 NCW conference she was made recording secretary and appointed to the committee of reference for resolutions. After joining the NCW's regional finance committee, she became national treasurer from 1898.

An accomplished speaker, Jessie Williamson was noted for 'her enthusiasm, and shrewd common sense'. She had a remarkably attractive personality and was very popular. A fellow worker recalled that 'The real wit of the gathering was Mrs Williamson. ... I have a clear picture of her merry face, amusing sallies and fluent Irish tongue. We all brightened up visibly when Mrs Williamson began to speak.' Her sense of humour was remarked upon most often and she was described as the Scobie Mackenzie of the women's parliament, after the witty Otago politician. In 1900 her photograph appeared on the cover of the *White Ribbon* with a caption describing her as 'one of the best-known and most widely-respected residents' of Wanganui.

Once the vote was won, the unity, visibility and optimism of the suffragists waned. By 1903 the Women's Political League was no longer meeting and the NCW was in decline. Williamson was one of the key women who kept much of the council's business going towards the end. She played a principal role in the last full conference at Napier in 1902, and in 1903, when the council was forced to limit itself to executive meetings only, was part of the six-woman deputation to Seddon on women's 'disabilities'.

At the 1902 conference, growing defensiveness became apparent – a symptom of the retreat of feminism in this period. Jessie Williamson argued that the council's objectives had been greatly misunderstood. Women who were alive to their responsibilities were called political women, and she was glad to be one of them. In a reversal of her earlier statements, she now claimed that there was no such thing as a woman's question; the aspirations of sisters and wives were of equal importance to those of brothers and husbands.

As well as organising on behalf of women, Williamson took an active interest in community welfare and the need for institutional reform. In 1896 she was appointed an official visitor to the female department of the Wanganui prison. She was struck forcibly by the state of the cells – 'inhuman places' – and the fact that women had little say in prison management.

She also attempted to get herself nominated onto the local
hospital board, believing that the involvement of women would
remedy widespread dissatisfaction with welfare administration.
She argued that the contemporary system of charitable aid
encouraged pauperism and that women should serve on all
local bodies dealing with relief distribution since this work was
essentially domestic, and would be easily performed by
women.

Despite Frances Stewart's success in gaining a seat on the
board in 1897, it took Williamson three years to become the
second Wanganui woman to do so. After making herself available to several borough and county councils, she was appointed
to the Patea and Wanganui United Charitable Aid Board
as a representative of the Wanganui Borough Council in
1900. In 1901 she petitioned Parliament for elective hospital
boards. From 1902 until she resigned in March 1904 she
represented the Marton Borough Council on the Wanganui
Hospital Board.

With Margaret Bullock, Jessie Williamson was deeply
involved in the ongoing debate over the appalling conditions
at Wanganui's Jubilee Home for the elderly. She was the
only hospital board member who visited the home and she
urged a proper system of classification of residents, a complete
change of management and the 'cultivation of a humanitarian
spirit'.

Her other concerns included illegitimacy and parental
responsibility. She had a strong belief in the need to protect the
young from corruption. Williamson denounced the sexual
double standard which put the burden of disgrace for illegitimate births on women, but not men, and argued that men
should be forced to acknowledge their role. Her solutions
included compelling every man to provide for his illegitimate
children according to his means, and aiding the mother in
establishing proof of paternity. Those children whose paternity
could not be proved and who could not be cared for, should be
brought up in cottage homes and trained by good men and
women to be useful members of society.

While Jessie Williamson shared many of the interests of her feminist contemporaries, she was wary of the temperance movement. She believed in temperance in all things but especially language: 'The rabid statements made by some temperance reformers really got her back up'. During her time in Wanganui Williamson was a member of the local SPCA, she founded a female court of the Ancient Order of Foresters of Wellington, and she displayed a keen interest in the local organisation of the conservative opposition.

Around 1904 the family moved to Linwood, Christchurch, where Hugh Williamson continued as a chemist. Jessie Williamson spoke at that year's public NCW meeting at Christchurch which was called to discuss Seddon's memorandum on 'Child-life preservation'. In 1905 she attended the council's final three-day executive session there.

Jessie Williamson's daughters Ann and Mary married, and in about 1909 the remaining members of the family moved to Hawera. Hugh set up business in High Street where another daughter, Sheila, also worked as a dentist. By 1919 the Williamsons were living in Remuera, Auckland, while Lena Williamson, a chemist, boarded at the Nurses' Home at Auckland Hospital.

Although Hugh had retired, Jessie became active once again on behalf of women. As a younger member of New Zealand's first wave of feminists, she was one of a handful of women, including Christina Henderson and Jessie Mackay, who provided a link to the new burst of activism. From 1916 to 1918 she attended meetings to form an Auckland branch of the revived NCW as a representative of the Civic League – a feminist organisation formed in 1913 to raise awareness of women's issues and support women's efforts to run for public office. She was a vice president of the new branch of the NCW from 1918 to 1919. She was also vice president of the Civic League in 1922 and from 1926 to 1928, and served on the executive from 1931 to 1932.

Hugh Williamson died in Auckland on 23 March 1926. After a lifetime of public feminist activity, which intensified

after her husband's death, Jessie Williamson died at her home
in Epsom, on 26 July 1937.

*Bronwyn Labrum*

Holt, B. *et al. Women in Council.* Wellington, 1980

Labrum, B. ' "For the better discharge of our duties": women's rights
in Wanganui, 1893–1903'. *Women's Studies Journal* 6, No 1/2 (1990):
136–152

'Woman, I think, should take her place alongside of man even in Parliament.
I think our Parliament would be very much better if we had
some women in it.' Elizabeth Yates in an interview
after her election as mayor of Onehunga in 1893.

# YATES, ELIZABETH
## *1840-48?-1918*

Elizabeth Oman was born in Caithness, Scotland, probably sometime between 1840 and 1848, the elder daughter of George Oman and his wife, Eleanor Lannigan. She arrived in Auckland, New Zealand, around December 1853 with her parents and sister Eleanor.

Little is known about her early life or education; her father worked as a labourer and the family appears to have lived in Onehunga at least from 1855 onwards. On 15 December 1875 at St Peter's Church, Onehunga, Elizabeth Oman married Michael Yates, a master mariner well known in the coastal trade. They lived in the family home at Selwyn Street with Elizabeth's widowed mother; there were no children of the marriage.

Michael Yates, a member of the Onehunga Borough Council since 1885, was elected mayor in 1888, holding office until 1892 when ill health led to his retirement. Elizabeth Yates assisted him with his duties throughout his incumbency. She was a strong supporter of women's suffrage and was the first woman to record her vote in the electorate under the new Electoral Act of 1893. She belonged to the Auckland Union Parliament and was a keen debater at its meetings.

In 1893 Elizabeth Yates accepted nomination for the office of mayor of Onehunga. She defeated her sole opponent, F. W. Court, at the election of 29 November, to become the first woman mayor in the British Empire. This radical departure from convention caused much comment throughout New Zealand and the empire, and Yates received congratulations from Premier Richard Seddon and Queen Victoria. The office also carried the appointment of justice of the peace. After being sworn in before Edward Conolly, judge of the Supreme Court, on 16 January 1894, she officiated occasionally as magistrate in cases involving women.

However, there was a hard core of local opposition to a woman filling these two traditionally male offices. Four councillors and the town clerk resigned immediately. Meetings were disrupted by unseemly altercations, and three councillors conducted an orchestrated policy of opposition to all proposals submitted by the mayor. Elizabeth Yates's tactless, dictatorial manner and partial disregard for established rules of procedure further exacerbated the situation. At times spectators crammed the small council chamber and interrupted proceedings, while outside the chamber unruly elements hooted and jeered. Newspapers published verbatim accounts of these 'disgraceful' scenes for the delectation of their readers.

On 28 November 1894 Mayor Yates was roundly defeated at the polls. Nevertheless, records show that much had been accomplished. She had liquidated the borough debt, established a sinking fund, reorganised the fire brigade, upgraded roads, footpaths and sanitation, and had personally lobbied the government to authorise the reopening of the Waikaraka cemetery. Even her enemies conceded that she had been an able administrator.

In September 1899 Elizabeth Yates made a triumphal return to the Onehunga Borough Council. She had lost none of her combativeness and was still forthright in expressing her opinions. She lost her seat in the election of April 1901.

Elizabeth Yates was admitted to Auckland Mental Hospital in November 1909 and died there on 6 September 1918. She was buried in St Peter's churchyard, Onehunga, beside her husband who had died in 1902. A pioneer in the participation of women in public life, Elizabeth Yates is assured of a place in the political history of New Zealand.

*Janice C. Mogford*

'Interview with Mrs Yates'. *New Zealand Graphic and Ladies' Journal.* 16 Dec. 1893

Mogford, J. C. *Onehunga: a brief history.* [Onehunga], 1977

Obit. *New Zealand Herald.* 9 Sept. 1918

# INDEX